PRAYERS AND POEMS OF INSPIRATION

*"Evening, and morning,
and at noon,
will I pray . . .
and he shall
hear my
voice."*

Psalm 54:17

IDEALS PUBLISHING CORPORATION
NASHVILLE, TENNESSEE

Foreword

In the two thousand years since its advent, Christianity has spread across the globe and found unique expression in every culture it has touched. One thing, however, has remained constant; Christians of all eras, all nations, and all churches have recognized their need for prayer. Prayer is a common bond that unites Christians across time, space, and denomination. The lives included in this volume represent a variety of Christian voices; their poems and prayers rise above the specific circumstances of their lives and speak to all persons who seek a closer communion with God.

ACKNOWLEDGMENTS

WITHOUT THIS FAITH from *Midstream* by Helen Keller, copyright © 1929 by The Crowell Publishing Company. GIVE ME A DREAM and OUR SECRET from *Adventures in Prayer* by Catherine Marshall, copyright © 1975 by Catherine Marshall. Published by Chosen Books, Fleming H. Revell Company. Used by permission. FOR RELEASE FROM RESENTMENT and WITH SORROW AND TRUE REPENTANCE from *The Prayers of Peter Marshall*, compiled and edited by Catherine Marshall, copyright © 1949, 1950, 1951, 1954 by Catherine Marshall. Renewed 1982. Published by Chosen Books, Fleming H. Revell Company. Used by Permission. THE ROAD AHEAD from *Thoughts in Solitude* by Thomas Merton, copyright © 1956, 1958 by the Abbey of Our Lady of Gethsemani. Renewal copyright © 1986 by the Trustees of the Thomas Merton Legacy Trust. Reprinted by permission of Farrar, Straus & Giroux, Inc. WE GIVE THEE THANKS: Thomas Merton: *Collected Poems of Thomas Merton*. Copyright © 1962 by The Abbey of Gethsemani, Inc. Reprinted by permission of New Directions Publishing Corporation. Excerpts from A LETTER by Lottie Moon, used by permission of Foreign Mission Board Records, Southern Baptist Historical Library and Archives, Nashville, Tennessee. FORGIVENESS by Corrie ten Boom, used by permission of Christians, Inc., Orange, California. A NEW START from the book *Each New Day* by Corrie ten Boom, copyright © 1977 by Corrie ten Boom. Used by permission of Fleming H. Revell Company.

Published by Ideals Publishing Corporation
565 Marriott Drive
Suite 800
Nashville, Tennessee 37214

Printed and bound in the United States of America.

ISBN 0-8249-4047-4

The text type was set in Goudy.
The display type was set in Shelley Allegro.
Color separations were made by Rayson Films of Waukesha, Wisconsin.
Printed and bound by Ringier America, New Berlin, Wisconsin.

Cover Photo: Cathedral of Notre Dame, Paris, France, H. Armstrong Roberts

Contents

Jesus and Prayer

"It is written,
my house shall
be called
the house
of prayer."

Matthew 11:13

Since the first settlers landed on the New England coast
more than three hundred and fifty years ago, residents of
the area have prayed together in small country churches
like this one in Sugar Hill, New Hampshire.

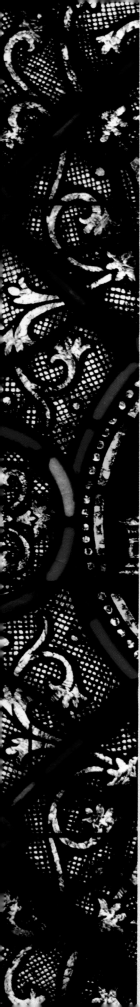

Jesus and Prayer

During His life, Jesus prayed and taught His followers about prayer. He explained that God, a loving Father, will give to His children, if they will only ask (Luke 11:5-13).

The Bible is full of examples of Jesus praying. He commanded that we pray for our enemies: "Pray for them, which despitefully use you, and persecute you; That ye may be the children of your Father which is in heaven" (Matthew 5:45). On the cross, Jesus prayed for those who persecuted Him: "Father, forgive them, for they know not what they do" (Luke 23:43). He also taught that prayer guards against temptation. During His final hours in the garden, Christ rebuked Peter for falling asleep and, knowing of Peter's upcoming temptation, suggested the following: "What, could ye not watch with me one hour? Watch and pray, that ye enter not into temptation; the spirit indeed is willing, but the flesh is weak" (Matthew 26:40-41). Jesus Himself prayed for Peter's strength: "the Lord said, 'Simon, Simon, behold, Satan hath desired to have you, that he may sift you as wheat: But I have prayed for thee, that thy faith fail not' " (Luke 22:31).

Jesus taught us to be persistent in our prayer: "Shall not God avenge His own elect, which cry day and night unto Him, though He bear long with them? I tell you that He will avenge them speedily" (Luke 18:7-8a). Many people worry about the posture of their bodies in prayer, but Jesus prayed kneeling (Luke 22:41), with His head on the ground (Matthew 26:39), and standing (John 11:41). His concern was with the posture of the spirit, which must be humble. We must be bold enough to approach God with our needs, but always so humble as to recognize our dependence. Jesus ends a parable with the admonition: "when thou prayest, enter into thy closet, and when thou hast shut thy door, pray to thy Father which is in secret; and thy Father which seeth in secret shall reward thee openly. . . . for your Father knoweth what things ye have need of before ye ask him" (Matthew 6:6-8).

The disciples asked Jesus, "Lord teach us to pray" (Luke 11:1). Jesus responded with parables, lessons, and His own examples, all of which help us understand how and why we must pray.

Ask, and It Shall Be Given

Ask, and it shall be given you;
seek, and ye shall find;
knock and it shall be opened unto you.

For every one that asketh receiveth:
and he that seeketh findeth:
and to him that knocketh
it shall be opened.

If a son shall ask bread
of any of you that is a father,
will he give him a stone?

Or if he ask a fish,
will he for a fish give him a serpent?
Or if he shall ask an egg,
will he offer him a scorpion?

If ye then, being evil,
know how to give good gifts
unto your children:

how much more
shall your heavenly Father
give the Holy Spirit
to them that ask Him?

Luke 11:5-13

In the Garden

Father, the hour is come;
glorify thy Son that thy Son may glorify thee:
as thou hast given him power over all flesh,
that he should give eternal life to as many as thou hast given him.

And this is life eternal, that they might know thee
the only true God, and Jesus Christ, whom thou has sent.
I have glorified thee on the earth:
I have finished the work which thou gavest me to do. . . .
Holy Father, keep through thine own name those whom thou hast
given me, that they may be one, as we are. While I was with them
in the world, I kept them in thy name: those that thou gavest me
I have kept, and none of them is lost. . . .

And the glory which thou gavest me I have given them;
that they may be one, even as we are one:
I in them, and thou in me, that they may be made perfect in one;
and that the world may know that thou hast sent me,
and hast loved them, as thou hast loved me.

Father, I will that they also, whom thou hast given me,
be with me where I am; that they may behold my glory, which
thou hast given me: for thou lovest me before the
foundation of the world.

O righteous Father, . . .
I have declared unto them thy name, and will declare it:
that the love wherewith thou hast loved me
may be in them, and I in them.

John 17

The best model for our own prayer is the example set by
Jesus himself. This stained glass from the First Presbyterian
Church in Port Angeles, Washington, depicts Jesus in a
classic posture of prayer to His Father.

The Lord's Prayer

Our Father
which art in heaven,
Hallowed
be thy name.

Thy kingdom come.
Thy will be done
in earth,
as it is in heaven.

Give us this day
our daily bread.
And forgive us our debts,
as we forgive our debtors.

And lead us not
into temptation,
but deliver us from evil:

For thine
is the kingdom,
and the power,
and the glory,
for ever.
Amen.

Matthew 6:9-13

In prayer we recognize the majesty of the Lord. Stained
glass windows like this one from Beverly Cathedral in
Beverly, England, are an example of man's artistic tribute
to that same majesty.

Lives of Compassionate Conviction

"Choose you
this day whom
ye will serve . . .
but as for me
and my house,
we will serve
the Lord"

Joshua 24:15

This small Wisconsin Church exemplifies the thousands of rural American churches that provide a place to worship and a sense of community for those living in our country's isolated regions.

Charles Dickens

Charles Dickens was born into unremarkable circumstances in Portsmouth, England, in 1812. His father, John Dickens, was an irresponsible parent and provider. His job as a payroll clerk for the navy required constant relocation, and his inability to manage his salary left his children often wanting. At the age of twelve, Charles was forced to go to work in a blacking factory attaching labels to jars of shoe polish in an attempt to bolster family finances. Dickens grew up determined not to live the life of hardship and uncertainty he had learned from his father.

Dickens held a variety of jobs in his early adulthood: law clerk, court reporter, and finally in 1834, reporter for the London *Morning Chronicle*. He enjoyed his work as a reporter, but he truly loved fiction writing. In 1836, Dickens contracted to write a series of humorous sketches called *The Pickwick Papers*. This work proved so successful that Dickens turned to fiction writing full time. Until his death in 1870, Dickens produced some of the most memorable fiction ever written, including *David Copperfield, Oliver Twist, Great Expectations*, and *A Christmas Carol*.

Dickens' writing brought success, but he was not satisfied to improve only his own life. The hardship and neglect he had known as a child inspired a lifetime commitment to helping children. While a reporter, Dickens helped influence the passing of a bill in the House of Lords that forbade employment of children under the age of thirteen in the factories. He also devoted his voice and his pen to the plight of orphaned children by working to improve their education.

Charles Dickens' novels are filled with phrases from the Bible and the Book of Common Prayer. He believed strongly in God and the Christian life but detested the divisiveness and politics that corrupted so many religious institutions. He believed Christianity should include charity, tolerance, and goodwill toward all humanity. These are the values that inspired Dickens to aid the poor and orphaned children, and these are the same values that resound in his prayers.

from Prayer of the Wiltshire Laborers

The God who took a little child,
And set him in the midst,
And promised him His mercy mild,
As by Thy Son, Thou didst;
Look down upon our children dear,
So gaunt, so cold, so spare,
And let their images appear,
Where lords and gentry are!

O God, teach them to feel how we,
When our poor infants droop,
Are weakened in our trust in Thee,
And how our spirits stoop;
For in Thy rest, so bright and fair,
All tears and sorrows sleep;
And their young looks, so full of care,
Would make the angels weep!

O God, remind them! In the bread
They break upon their knee,
Those sacred words may yet be read
"In Memory of Me!"
O God, remind them of His sweet
Compassion for the poor,
And how He gave them bread to eat,
And went from door to door!

Charles Dickens

A Child's Prayer

Hear my prayer, O Heavenly Father,
Ere I lay me down to sleep;
Bid Thy angels, pure and holy
Round my bed their vigils keep.

My sins are heavy but Thy mercy
Far outweighs them every one;
Down before Thy cross I cast them,
Trusting in Thy help alone.

Keep me through this night of peril
Underneath its boundless shade;
Take me to Thy rest, I pray Thee,
When my pilgrimage is made.

None shall measure out Thy patience
By the span of human thought;
None shall bound Thy tender mercies
Which Thy holy Son has bought.

Pardon all my past transgressions,
Give me strength for days to come;
Guide and guard me with Thy blessing
Till Thy angels bid me home.

Charles Dickens

Charles Dickens' wish was that no child would face the
hardship he knew as a young boy growing up in poverty
and working in the factories in London. Wells Cathedral,
seen here nestled in the rolling green countryside, repre-
sents a side of British life that Dickens could only dream
about as a boy and that appeared often in his novels.

John Donne

John Donne's life is crisply divided: a wild early life, a difficult mid-life, and a rich and successful later life. Throughout his entire life, Donne wrote verses, but only upon his surrender to God and King James did he achieve fulfillment.

Donne was born in 1572 into a Roman Catholic family in Elizabethan London at a time of Catholic persecution. He attended both Oxford and Cambridge Universities and trained for the law, but he took no degree and never practiced law. In his youth, he traveled a great deal, fought against the Spaniards, and courted a multitude of ladies. In short, he was a brilliant rogue.

Intelligent and educated but dependent on the patronage of the wealthy and the nobility, Donne received an appointment as secretary to Sir Thomas Egerton, an official in Queen Elizabeth's court. Three years later, Donne secretly married Egerton's seventeen-year-old niece. When Egerton discovered the marriage, he not only dismissed Donne, but had him jailed as well. Nonetheless, the marriage was a happy one.

In his mid-thirties, Donne underwent a period in which he was poor, sick, and unhappy. During this time, he turned to the Anglican church. For some inexplicable reason, King James was adamant that Donne should be a preacher; and Donne found only closed doors to employment in any other field. Donne finally relented and entered the ministry in 1615. In six years, he became dean of London's St. Paul's Cathedral. In the pulpit, Donne called upon his education, his wit, and his flamboyance. As the king had suspected, Donne became a great preacher, and his fame increased each year until his death in 1631.

In his youth, Donne wrote passionate verses on love. After his marriage, the passion remained in his poetry, but the focus shifted from the physical to the metaphysical. By the time he entered the ministry, he was writing only religious verses; in his later years, he gave up poetry altogether and wrote only sermons. Donne produced a body of work rich in life's experiences that speaks to us yet today. The heartfelt words are those of a brilliant man with whom God was patient until he could declare ". . . for I, except You enthrall me, never shall be free."

Sonnet

Batter my heart three-personed God;
for You as yet but knock, breathe, shine,
and seek to mend;
that I may rise, and stand,
o'erthrow me, and bend
Your force, to break, blow, burn,
and make me new.

I, like an usurp'd town,
to another due,
labor to admit You, but O, to no end,
reason Your viceroy in me,
me should defend,
but is captived,
and proves weak or untrue.

Yet dearly I love You,
and would be loved fain,
but am betrothed unto Your enemy:

Divorce me,
untie or break the knot again,
take me to You, imprison me, for I,
except You enthrall me,
never shall be free,
nor ever chaste,
except You ravish me.

John Donne

A Hymn to God the Father

Wilt Thou forgive that sin where I begun,
Which is my sin, though it were done before?
Wilt Thou forgive that sin, through which I run,
And do run still: though still I do deplore?
When Thou hast done, Thou hast not done,
For I have more.

Wilt Thou forgive that sin by which I have won
Others to sin? and made my sin their door?
Wilt Thou forgive that sin which I did shun
A year or two; but wallowed in a score?
When Thou hast done, Thou hast not done,
For I have more.

I have a sin of fear, that when I have spun
My last thread, I shall perish on the shore;
Swear by Thyself, that at my death Thy Son
Shall shine as He shines now, and heretofore;
And, having done that, Thou hast done,
I fear no more.

John Donne

St. Paul's Cathedral in London was the scene of John
Donne's greatest sermons. The original Gothic cathedral
was destroyed by the Great Fire of 1666. The great domed
cathedral that stands on the site today was designed and
built by Sir Christopher Wren between 1675 and 1710.
Inside is an impressive effigy of former Dean of St. Paul's
John Donne, one of the few surviving elements from the
original cathedral.

John Henry Newman

John Henry Newman was born into a London banker's family in 1801. He graduated from Oxford University at nineteen and four years later was ordained an Anglican clergyman. Newman quickly rose to prominence due to his forceful sermons and charismatic presence. He was so respected that he became a leader of the Oxford Movement, an attempt to return the Church of England to its conservative roots.

To all outward observers, John Henry Newman was confident and secure in his faith when, at the suggestion of friends and doctors who noticed his failing health, he traveled to Italy in the hope that the mild climate might offer healing. What his friends and doctors did not realize was that the deterioration of his physical health was the outward manifestation of an internal sickness. John Henry Newman, born and raised an Anglican and one of his church's bright young leaders, had become uncertain of his religion.

Italy did not improve John Henry Newman's physical health, but conversations he had there with Catholic leaders eased his heart and mind. In 1845, at the age of forty-four, Newman became a Roman Catholic. In 1847, he was ordained a priest. When Newman returned to England, he left Oxford and moved to Birmingham, where he lived to the age of eighty-nine, preaching, teaching, and writing. He was elevated to the rank of cardinal in 1879.

Newman's prayers and poems reveal a spiritual faith strengthened through reason. His works are marked by beautiful language, sensitivity of spirit, and complete dedication to God.

Praise to the Holiest

Praise to the Holiest in the height,
And in the depths be praise;
In all His words most wonderful,
Most sure in all His ways. . . .

O loving wisdom of our God!
When all was sin and shame,
A second Adam to the fight
And to the rescue came.

O wisest love! that flesh and blood,
Which did in Adam fail,
Should strive afresh against the foe,
Should strive and should prevail;

And that a higher gift than grace
Should flesh and blood refine;
God's presence and His very self,
An essence all-divine.

O generous love! Thee who smote
In man, for man, the foe,
The double agony in man,
For man, should undergo;

And in the garden secretly,
And on the cross on high
Should teach His brethren and inspire
To suffer and to die.

Praise to the Holiest in the height,
And in the depths be praise;
In all His words most wonderful,
Most sure in all His ways.

John Henry Newman

Prayer

O Lord,
support us all the day long,
until the shadows lengthen
and the evening comes,
and the busy world is hushed,
and the fever of life is over,
and our work is done.

Then, Lord,
in Your mercy
grant us safe lodging,
and a holy rest,
and peace at the last;
through Jesus Christ
our Lord.
Amen.

John Henry Newman

When John Henry Newman made the decision to leave the Church of England and convert to Catholicism, he also decided to leave Oxford, which was too closely associated with his Anglican past. Newman spent his years after the 1845 conversion in the city Birmingham in Warwickshire. Pictured is the Birmingham Cathedral, located in the city center.

John Keble

Born in Gloucestershire, England, in April of 1792, John Keble dreamed his entire life of becoming a clergyman. Tutored in childhood by his father, an Anglican clergyman himself, John was a brilliant student who earned high honors at Oxford. He achieved his lifelong dream at the age of twenty-four when he was ordained a priest in the Church of England. Before his death in 1866, John Keble also achieved fame as a professor, a poet, and a leader of a movement to reform the Anglican church.

John Keble was a sensitive and pious man. His mind was continually occupied with the search for religious truth, and he wrote poetry as a means of revealing the spiritual meaning behind everyday experiences. In 1827, he published a volume of religious poetry and hymns called *The Christian Year*. The book achieved international recognition and helped gain Keble the post of professor of poetry at Oxford.

At Oxford, Keble was destined for even greater fame as a leader of the Oxford Movement, a crusade to return the Anglican church to its traditional roots. In a university sermon delivered in July of 1833, Keble declared that the church had become too liberal and was in danger of losing its identity and strength. His goal was not to destroy the Anglican church nor to split it apart; Keble simply hoped to prevent the church from losing sight of its true purpose.

John Keble believed that the only truth was religious truth. Anything that threatened to obscure that truth threatened the existence of man. Unlike some great poets who were also ministers, John Keble never felt that there was a conflict between his religious life and his poetry. For him, poetry was the truest form of expression, and religion the most worthy subject matter.

from Fourth Sunday after Easter

My Saviour, can it ever be
That I should gain by losing Thee?
The watchful mother tarries nigh
Though sleep has closed her infant's eye,
For should he wake and find her gone,
She knows she could not bear his moan.
But I am weaker than a child,
And Thou art more than mother dear;
Without Thee heaven were but a wild;
How can I live without Thee here?

"Tis good for you that I should go,
You lingering yet awhile below"—
Tis Thine own gracious promise, Lord!
Thy saints have proved the faithful word,
When heaven's bright boundless avenue
Far opened on their eager view,
And homeward to Thy Father's throne,
Still lessening, brightening on their sight
Thy shadowy car went soaring on,
They tracked Thee up th'abyss of light.

Thou bidd'st rejoice; they dare not mourn,
But to their home in gladness turn,
Their home and God's, that favored place
Where still He shines on Abraham's race,
In prayers and blessings there to wait
Like supplicants at their monarch's gate
Who, bent with bounty rare to aid
The splendor of His crowning day,
Keeps back awhile His largess made
More welcome for that brief delay.

John Keble

from Second Sunday after Christmas

And wilt Thou hear the fever'd heart
To Thee in silence cry?
And as the inconstant wild fires dart
Out of the restless eye,
Wilt Thou forgive the wayward thought
By kindly woes yet half untaught
A Saviour's right, so dearly bought,
That hope should never die?

Thou wilt; for Thou art Israel's God,
And Thine unwearied arm
Is ready yet with Moses' rod,
The hidden rill to charm
Out of the dry, unfathomed deep
Of sands, that lie in lifeless sleep,
Save when the scorching whirlwinds heap
Their waves in rude alarm.

John Keble

Christ Church College, pictured at left, is one of the thirty-five colleges in the city of Oxford, England, that make up Oxford University. The great poets and public figures of Britain have been educated at Oxford for eight hundred years. John Keble studied here as a young man, but he achieved his greatest fame as an Oxford professor and a leader of the movement to force the Anglican church back to its traditional roots.

Lives of Perseverance and Sufferance

"Blessed are they which are persecuted for righteousness' sake: for theirs is the kingdom of heaven."

Matthew 5:10

The Moravians came to America from Europe in the eighteenth century seeking relief from religious persecution. They settled first in Georgia, then moved on to Bethlehem, Pennsylvania, and Salem, North Carolina. Pictured is a Moravian church in Lititz, Pennsylvania.

Corrie ten Boom

Corrie ten Boom is one of the most inspirational figures of the twentieth century, a woman who answered the world's cruelty and suffering with forgiveness and faith. Born in 1892 in Amsterdam, Holland, Corrie was one of four children of Cor and Caspar ten Boom. Her father was a watchmaker, a job which provided barely enough income to support his family. Her mother was a kind and generous person who took what little income there was and managed to make a home, not only for her own family, but for all who needed their help. The ten Booms taught their children by lesson and example to lead Christian lives of kindness and caring.

Perhaps the most important lesson in Corrie ten Boom's childhood came after her heart was broken in a typical teenage crush. As a young girl, Corrie was swept off her feet by a friend of her brother. Her brother warned that his friend's plans did not include a poor girl like Corrie, but her romantic longings would not let her believe this fact. When the friend arrived at the ten Boom home to introduce his fiance, Corrie was crushed. She looked to her father for comfort; what he offered was God. Caspar ten Boom told his daughter to ask God for the strength to love this man who had broken her heart, not with fragile, human love, but with the love that God himself has for His children, a love full of forgiveness. Corrie ten Boom remembered this lesson throughout the remainder of a life full of pain and hardship.

Corrie ten Boom saw her family destroyed by the Nazis, and she herself suffered long months in a concentration camp. Through it all, she never forgot the lesson of her childhood. An all-forgiving love became the foundation of her life. She forgave the man who betrayed her family to the Nazis for harboring Jewish refugees, she forgave the guards who humiliated her in the camps, and she forgave the nurse who mistreated her sister. At a time when war had spread pain and suffering across the world, Corrie ten Boom preached forgiveness and love. She became a world-renowned speaker and turned the lesson of her childhood into a worldwide ministry which awakened countless hearts to the truth that only by emulating God's love in our lives can we welcome Jesus into our hearts.

Forgiveness

When we forgive others
we often bury the hatchet,
leaving the handle out:
ready for future use.

God does not.
He blots out our sins like a cloud;
you never see a cloud again
once it has evaporated.

We are on the Lord's side
and thus are yoke-fellows with Jesus,
so we can face the foe,
being more than conquerors
through Him who loves us.

Do not ask:
"Can I be kept from sinning
if I keep close to Him?"

But rather:
"Can I be kept from sinning
if He keeps close to me?"

Corrie ten Boom

A New Start

Lord Jesus,
at the start of this new year,
we ask for a fresh beginning.
Wipe our sins away
with your precious blood.

Cleanse our hearts
of bitterness toward others.
Help us
to live each day
in close communion
with You,
our true and faithful guide.
Amen.

Corrie ten Boom

Corrie ten Boom moved to Haarlem, Holland, from Amsterdam when she was six months old after her father Caspar ten Boom took over his father's Haarlem watch shop. As a child, she received religious instruction at home from her parents and also at St. Bavo's Cathedral, pictured here.

Catherine Marshall

Catherine Marshall is known to us due to the tragic loss of her husband. Had she not been the wife of Senate Chaplain Peter Marshall and had not her husband met with an early and sudden death, Catherine Marshall may have led a quiet, anonymous life. Her marriage to Peter Marshall, however, thrust her into the public eye and gave her the opportunity to touch the world with her faith.

Catherine Wood Marshall was born in West Virginia. The daughter of a Presbyterian minister, Catherine had a happy and somewhat sheltered childhood. She attended the all-female Agnes Scott College, training to become a teacher. Shortly before her graduation, however, she met Peter Marshall, a young minister at an Atlanta church. After a brief courtship, they were married; Catherine abandoned her plans to teach and assumed the role of wife and mother. She lived, as did most women of her generation, in the shadow of her husband, a great man loved and respected by all who knew him.

On the morning of January 25, 1949, Catherine Marshall received a phone call that ended the life she knew. Her husband had died, leaving her alone without money, without experience in caring for herself and her young son, and without direction. Marshall sank into grief, and there she found God. She gave herself and her pain and her uncertainties to Him. She looked to God to help her find a way to continue, not just emotionally and spiritually, but practically as well. She prayed constantly, not asking for special favors and relief, but for guidance and strength.

After her husband's death, Catherine Marshall established a career as a writer and editor. With no practical experience, she compiled several books of her husband's sermons, wrote his biography, and oversaw its production as a film. She also made speeches and wrote about her own life and experiences. She shared the story of her difficult times; when she had seen no future for herself, she asked God to guide her, and He did. Catherine Marshall spread the message that God has not abandoned His people; if those who need strengthening seek and follow Him, He will act in the events of our everyday lives.

Give Me a Dream

Father,
once—it seems long ago now—
I had such big dreams,
so much anticipation of the future.
Now no shimmering horizon beckons me;
my days are lackluster.
I see so little of lasting value in the daily round.
Where is Your plan for my life, Father?

You have told us that without vision, we men perish.
So Father in heaven,
knowing that I can ask in confidence
for what is Your expressed will to give me,
I ask You to deposit in my mind and heart the particular dream,
the special vision You have for my life.

And along with the dream,
will You give me whatever graces, patience,
and stamina it takes
to see the dream through to fruition?
I sense that this may involve adventures
I have not bargained for,
but I want to trust You enough to follow
even if You lead along new paths.
I admit to liking some of my ruts.
But I know that habit patterns
that seem like cozy nests from the inside,
from Your vantage point may be prison cells.
Lord, if You have to break down any prisons of mine
before I can see the stars and catch the vision,
then Lord, begin the process now.
In joyous expectation,
Amen.

Catherine Marshall

Our Secret

Father, I begin to see that
You have decreed the Law of Secrecy all
through Your Creation. Seeds secreted in the warm earth
are invisible to all eyes but Yours during the long days
of germination. Baby chicks hidden in the eggs
do not cackle or crow during the weeks of incubation
beneath the patient mother hen.
Our creation too requires the months of seclusion
in the dark of the womb.
So I see that prayer, the highest form of creation,
must also for a time be hidden with You
for Your work to be accomplished.

Lord, here is a request dear to my heart.
It strengthens my faith to know that You want this petition
to be our secret; that as I hide my request in You,
I have touched the creative heart of the universe.
So I leave this prayer with You, Father.
As day follows day with no results visible to me,
give me the gift of knowing that since You care for me
more tenderly than for any seeds or eggs,
Your work of Creation on my behalf
is going on just as surely.
How I thank You! In the beauty and strength
of Jesus' name I pray.
Amen.

Catherine Marshall

This stained glass is from the interior of the National
Cathedral in Washington D.C., where Catherine Marshall
heard her husband Peter deliver sermons during his tenure
as Senate Chaplain. Also known as the Cathedral Church
of St. Peter and St. Paul, the National Cathedral was pat-
terned after Europe's fourteenth-century Gothic cathe-
drals. Construction of the cathedral began in 1907 and
was not completed until 1991.

John Milton

It is said of John Milton that as a student he read everything published in English, Latin, or Greek and knew the Bible by heart. This may be an exaggeration, but it is likely not far from true; Milton approached his studies with unusual discipline and devotion. He took the same approach to religion, and his deeply held Puritan beliefs gave a strong sense of purpose to his life.

Born in 1608, Milton revealed his intellectual curiosity early. At St. Paul's School, he learned Latin, Hebrew, Greek, and most of the modern European languages. He graduated from Christ's College, Cambridge, in 1629 with a Bachelor of Arts degree and in 1632 with a Master of Arts degree. For six years following graduation, Milton remained at his father's house and read everything available. In 1638, his father sent him on tour to the Continent where he remained for a year visiting the treasures of European museums.

In 1649, the Puritan government of Oliver Cromwell took control of England. Milton, a Puritan in both religion and politics, was appointed Latin Secretary. In 1651, he began to lose his eyesight; within a year, he was totally blind. He was able, however, to continue his duties in the government until 1660, when the monarchy of England was restored. Upon the Restoration, Milton was imprisoned and would have been executed, except for the intervention of friends. In the end, he was fined and all of his property confiscated.

For the remainder of his life, Milton returned to writing poetry and in total blindness dictated his greatest works: *Paradise Lost*, *Paradise Regained*, and *Samson Agonistes*. In these masterpieces, Milton draws on a lifetime of rich experiences: the Bible, the world's literature, the European Renaissance, his government's turmoil, and the Reformation. Most of all, however, he draws upon his own private struggles. These struggles challenged his faith and devotion to God, but Milton endured to profess his faith in both his epic works of literature and his humble, devout prayers.

Adam's Morning Prayer

These are Thy glorious works,
Parent of Good,
Almighty, Thine this universal frame,
thus wondrous fair;
Thyself how wondrous then!

Unspeakable, who sit'st
above these Heavens
to us invisible,
or dimly seen in these Thy lowest works;
yet these declare Thy goodness beyond thought,
and power divine.
Speak ye who best can tell,
ye sons of light.

Angels; for ye behold Him,
and with songs and choral symphonies,
day without night,
circle His throne rejoicing!
Ye in heaven;
on earth join all ye creatures
to extol Him first,
Him last,
Him midst,
and without end.

John Milton

When I Consider

When I consider how my light is spent,
Ere half my days, in this dark world and wide,
And that one talent which is death to hide
Lodged with me useless, though my soul more bent
To serve therewith my Maker, and present
My true account, lest He returning chide.

Doth God exact day-labour, light denied?
I fondly ask; but Patience, to prevent
That murmur soon replies: God doth not need
Either man's work or His own gifts; who best
Bear His mild yoke, they serve Him best. His state
Is kingly. Thousands at His bidding speed
And post o'er land and ocean without rest;
They also serve who only stand and wait.

John Milton

The Jesse Tree, depicted here in stained glass from All Saint's Cathedral in London, was a popular subject of medieval church art. The tree traces the lineage of Jesus back to David, the son of Jesse. John Milton also made use of biblical history for his art, turning the story of the Garden of Eden and man's fall from grace into *Paradise Lost*, one of the great epic poems in the history of the English language.

William Cowper

Although William Cowper's quiet voice spoke passionately of God and faith, his voice arose not from a bold and confident soul but from a life overwhelmed by the world. Tormented by mental illness most of his life, Cowper lived not among the great thinkers of his era, but in a quiet country home. Nonetheless, his simple message of Christianity speaks as powerfully as any.

Cowper was born in England in 1731. At the age of six, his mother died, and he was sent to boarding school. It was here that he began to feel different from other children. The teasing of the boys frightened young William, and he never felt at ease among his classmates. Insecurity and fear continued into law school, and he was never successful at the law or at any other public office.

His depression continued until he was institutionalized for a time; his only comfort came from religion and the Bible. Upon leaving the asylum, Cowper went to live in Olney at the request of evangelist John Newton. The two collaborated on the famous *Olney Hymns*, but Cowper suffered a second attack of madness in 1773. From that time on, he seldom left his home. He searched for any diversion for his mind in an attempt to hold onto his sanity. He tended his garden, cared for his pets, and tried his hand at carpentry; at the suggestion of a friend, he finally turned to poetry. The poems he wrote depicting the simple, English country life are his greatest works.

Cowper's religious verses hardly suggest an author who struggled with mental illness throughout his life. They speak of a peaceful heart, comfortable with and comforted by an abiding faith. Cowper never achieved a complete cure; depression and illness recurred until his death in 1800. Another constant companion, however, was his faith, which provided comfort while it inspired positive, life-affirming poetry.

Walking with God

Oh! for a closer walk with God,
A calm and heavenly frame;
A light to shine upon the road
That leads me to the Lamb!

Where is the blessedness I knew
When first I saw the Lord?
Where is the soul-refreshing view
Of Jesus and His word?

What peaceful hours I once enjoyed!
How sweet their memory still!
But they have left an aching void
The world can never fill.

Return, O Holy Dove, return,
Sweet messenger of rest;
I hate the sins that made Thee mourn,
And drove Thee from my breast.

The dearest idol I have known,
Whate'er that idol be,
Help me to tear it from Thy throne,
And worship only Thee.

So shall my walk be close with God,
Calm and serene my frame;
So purer light shall mark the road
That leads me to the Lamb.

William Cowper

Joy and Peace in Believing

Sometimes a light surprises
The Christian when he sings;
It is the Lord who rises
With healing on His wings.
When comforts are declining,
He brands the soul again
A season of clear shining
To cheer it after rain.

In holy contemplation
We sweetly then pursue
The theme of God's salvation,
And find it ever new.
Set free from present sorrow,
We cheerfully can say,
Let the unknown tomorrow
Bring with it what it may!

It can bring with it nothing
But He will bear us through;
Who gives the lilies clothing
Will clothe His people too.
Beneath the spreading heavens
No creature but is fed;
And He who feeds the ravens
Will give His children bread.

William Cowper

Olney, located on England's Ouse River, offered William Cowper a brief respite from his mental illness in the late 1760s when he traveled there to collaborate with the evangelical preacher John Newton on the *Olney Hymns*. Olney is also the site of the Parish Church of St. Peter's and St. Paul's, pictured at right.

Lives of Charitable Service

"Inasmuch as ye have done it unto one of the least of these my brethren, ye have done it unto me."

Matthew 25:40

Simple yet striking, this white frame church stands in a small town center. Like countless other houses of worship, its presence in the middle of town serves as an everyday reminder to residents of their duties to God and their fellow man.

Robert Louis Stevenson

The parents of Robert Louis Stevenson, author of the beloved children's tales *Treasure Island* and *Kidnapped*, never imagined their son would become a writer. The only son of Scottish Calvinists, Stevenson was expected to follow in the footsteps of his father, grandfather, and two uncles, all prominent civil engineers in Edinburgh. If it had not been for tuberculosis, which made Stevenson weak and unfit for the disciplined academic life of a future engineer, he may well have followed those footsteps; but his body's weakness relieved him from the burden of his family's expectations and left him free to envision his own future. What he saw was the life of a writer.

As a young man in Scotland, Stevenson published several essays and a book, but none brought him much acclaim. In addition, the cold, damp, Scottish air exacerbated his tuberculosis. At the age of thirty, Stevenson, still unknown as a writer, married. With his wife, he spent the next decade traveling the globe in search of a climate that might offer him relief. It was during these years that he had his first successes as a writer; *Treasure Island, A Child's Garden of Verse,* and *Dr. Jekyll and Mr. Hyde* were all written during Stevenson's years of travel.

Despite this growing success as an author, Stevenson still lacked a home. In 1889, his family and he finally found that home on the island of Upola in Samoa. Stevenson spent only five years on Samoa before he died in 1894 at the age of forty-four. In those five years, he devoted himself to the people of his adopted homeland. Stevenson had a special affection for the people of Samoa; he cherished their native culture and defended it against the destruction brought by British and German settlers. When Stevenson died, the Samoan people expressed their love for him by clearing a path through the jungle to the summit of Mt. Vaca, where Stevenson had asked to be buried.

While alive, Stevenson shared his strong Christian faith by writing prayers for those Samoans who had accepted Christ into their lives. The prayers he wrote for the people of Samoa are comforting reminders to all Christians of God's presence in our everyday lives.

Evensong

The embers of the day are red
Beyond the murky hill.
The kitchen smokes: the bed
In the darkened house is spread:
The great sky darkens overhead,
And the great woods are shrill.

So far have I been led,
Lord, by Thy will:
So far have I followed,
Lord, and wondered still.

The breeze from the embalmed land
Blows sudden toward the shore,
And claps my cottage door.
I hear the signal,
Lord—I understand.
The night at Thy command comes.
I will eat and sleep
And will not question more.

Robert Louis Stevenson

Family Prayer

Lord, behold our family here assembled.
We thank You for this place in which we dwell,
for the love that unites us,
for the peace accorded us this day,
for the hope with which we expect the morrow;
for the health, the work, the food and the bright skies
that make our lives delightful;
for our friends in all parts of the earth.

Give us courage and gaiety and the quiet mind.
Spare us to our friends, soften us to our enemies.
Bless us, if it may be, in all our innocent endeavors;

if it may not, give us the strength
to endure what is to come
that we may be brave in peril,
constant in tribulation, temperate in wrath
and in all changes of fortune
and down to the gates of death,
loyal and loving to one another.
as the clay to the potter,
as the windmill to the wind,
as children of their sire,
we beseech of You this help and mercy
for Christ's sake.
Amen.

Robert Louis Stevenson

This stained glass window from St. Andrew's Church in Great Fencote, England, presents a classic depiction of Jesus surrounded by children. Robert Louis Stevenson shared Jesus' special affection for young people. Although he had no children of his own, the wonderful Scottish storyteller wrote novels and stories that have been treasured by children worldwide for generations.

Helen Keller

Helen Keller, American author and crusader for the handicapped, was born in Tuscumbia, Alabama, in June of 1880. She lived her first nineteen months as a "normal" child before a serious illness took away her sight, hearing, and speech. Arthur and Kate Keller tried for the next several years to care for their helpless little girl, but she made no progress. In desperation, they appealed to the Perkins Institute for the Blind in Boston. It was to be the best decision they ever made for their child.

The Perkins Institute sent a young Irish-American woman named Annie Sullivan to Tuscumbia to work with seven-year-old Helen. Sullivan's inspired teaching quickly broke through Helen's darkness. Before long, Helen understood the basics of language and communication. Eventually, Helen learned to read, write, and speak. Annie Sullivan accompanied Helen to the Cambridge School for Young Ladies, where she sat by her student and translated each lecture into the language of touch. In 1900, Helen went on to Radcliffe College with Annie Sullivan once again at her side. Four years later, Helen graduated with honors. After completing her education, she became a committed spokeswomen for the handicapped, raising both money and public awareness. She also wrote several books, including an autobiography, *The Story of My Life*, and her example served as an inspiration for all Americans with obstacles to overcome.

As a young girl, Helen Keller was blessed with the friendship of Bishop Phillips Brooks, a man known for his special relationship with children. He answered her questions about God and religion and helped instill in her the love of God that would stay with her throughout her life. In *The Story of My Life*, Helen Keller explains the faith that Brooks fostered in her as a child. He "taught me no special creed or dogma; but he impressed upon my mind two great ideas—the fatherhood of God and the brotherhood of man . . . God is love, God is our Father; we are his children; therefore the darkest clouds will break, and though right be worsted, wrong shall not triumph." This simple faith guided Helen Keller through darkness unimaginable to most and allowed her to transform her life from helplessness to inspiration.

Without This Faith

Without this faith
there would be little meaning in my life.
I should be
"a mere pillar of darkness in the dark."

Observers in the full enjoyment
of their bodily senses pity me,
but it is because
they do not see
the golden chamber in my life
where I dwell delighted;
for, dark as my path may seem to them,
I carry a magic light in my heart.

Faith,
the spiritual strong searchlight,
illumines the way,
and although sinister doubts lurk in the shadow,
I walk unafraid
towards the Enchanted Wood
where the foliage is always green,
where joy abides,
where nightingales nest and sing,
and where life and death are one
in the presence of the Lord.

Helen Keller

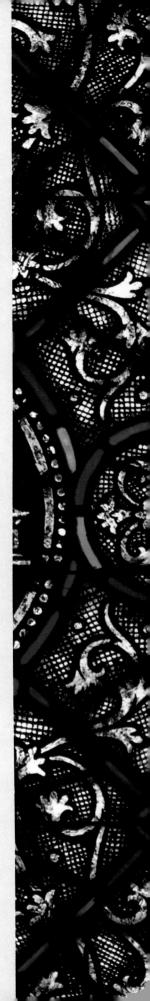

from The Story of My Life

The hands of those I meet
are dumbly eloquent to me . . . .
Others there are whose hands
have sunbeams in them,
so that their grasp warms my heart . . . .

I am too happy in this world
to think much about the future,
except that to remember that
I have cherished friends awaiting me
there in God's beautiful Somewhere.

In spite of the lapse of years,
they seem so close to me
that I should not think it strange
if at any moment
they should clasp my hand
and speak words of endearment
as they used to before they went away.

Helen Keller

Helen Keller never saw the beautiful light and color of
stained glass windows such as this one in the Cathedral of
St. John the Baptist in Savannah, Georgia. Nonetheless,
she came to know the beauty of God's spirit, thanks to her
own strong faith and to the kindness and commitment of
such friends as Phillips Brooks, Oliver Wendall Holmes,
and John Greenleaf Whittier, all of whom shared their
own vision with the brilliant, sightless Keller.

George Herbert

George Herbert lived a life of quiet faith and service and died never having published a single poem. Yet the literary world now honors this quietly intense writer as one of the greatest seventeenth-century poets.

Herbert was born into a wealthy English family in 1593. He was the youngest of five sons, and his father died while he was still a boy. Herbert graduated from Cambridge University with distinction and was elected Public Orator of the university. He served as a member of Parliament in the early 1620s; but because this career required patronage, Herbert followed the tradition of many younger sons of the time and took Anglican religious orders. Many people viewed the church as an easy means of guaranteeing a living, but Herbert took his position as pastor in the country parish of Bremerton very seriously.

He devoted his life to the people of Bremerton; he used his own money to rebuild the church, and he became a familiar figure in the homes of his parishioners, especially the sick, poor, and troubled. Although he was only in his post for three years before he died of consumption in 1633, Herbert was revered by his parishioners, who took to calling him "Holy Mr. Herbert" in honor of his humility, kindness, and charity.

In his years at Bremerton, Herbert privately wrote poetry as an aid to his preaching and prayer. Shortly after his death a single volume, *The Temple*, was published by a friend. Herbert's poems use simple language and common imagery to touch all aspects of the life of a Christian believer, from the despair of doubt to the joy of true faith. The volume is a spiritual biography and depicts the inner life of a man devoted to serving God. George Herbert only lived forty years; he saw little of the world and achieved no great fame during his lifetime. His life is proof that intense Christian faith need not be proven by drama or public words; it may simply be expressed in the quiet ministrations of a life of service and contemplation.

Love

Love bade me welcome; yet my soul drew back,
Guilty of dust and sin.
But quick-eyed Love, observing me grow slack
From my first entrance in,
Drew nearer to me, sweetly questioning,
If I lacked anything.

"A guest," I answered, "worthy to be here:"
Love said, "You shall be he."
"I, the unkind, ungrateful? Ah, my dear,
I cannot look on Thee."
Love took my hand, and smiling did reply,
"Who made the eyes but I?"

"Truth Lord, but I have marred them; let my shame
Go where it doth deserve."
"And know you not," says Love, "who bore the blame?"
"My dear, then I will serve."
"You must sit down," says Love, "and taste my meat."
So I did sit and eat.

George Herbert

Easter Wings

Lord, who createst man in wealth and store,
Though foolishly he lost the same,
Decaying more and more
Till he became
Most poor:
With Thee
O let me rise
As larks, harmoniously,
And sing this day Thy victories:
Then shall that fall further the flight in me.

My tender age in sorrow did begin:
And still with wickedness and shame
Thou didst so punish sin,
That I became
Most thin.
With Thee
Let me combine,
And feel this day Thy victory;
For, if I imp my wing on Thine,
Affliction shall advance the flight in me.

George Herbert

George Herbert's "Easter Wings" is an example of "shaped verse," a traditional form of poetry in which the appearance of the words and lines on the page is a symbolic representation of the poem's subject. The lines of this poem form the shape of wings, signifying the uplifting power of God's grace. The same symbol is found in this stained glass window from St. Joseph's College in Mill Hill, England.

Oliver Wendell Holmes

Oliver Wendell Holmes' life was one of service. Born in 1809 into a privileged Boston family, Holmes was not content to live on the wealth and name of his family. As a respected doctor and one of America's most beloved poets, he worked throughout his life to improve the quality of life for all mankind.

The son of a Congregational minister and the grandson of both a surgeon and a judge, Holmes inherited the family drive for achievement. As a young man, he matriculated at Harvard, where he excelled in academics and also earned the title of Class Poet at the age of twenty. After graduation, Holmes briefly pursued a career in law but decided that his true calling was medicine. He attended medical school first in Paris and then at Harvard. Meanwhile, he continued to write poetry. The year he graduated from Harvard Medical School was also the year he published his first volume of poetry.

For the remainder of his life, Dr. Holmes continued to balance his creative and scientific sides; he became a member of the American literary elite and a respected doctor who was eventually appointed Dean of Harvard Medical School. In both medicine and literature, Holmes was known as an intelligent, devoted, and ethical man, concerned with the quality and honesty of his work. Dr. Holmes was never afraid to tell the truth, whether it meant reminding his fellow doctors that their unsanitary procedures often spread the very diseases they labored to cure or satirizing the grandiose posturing of his literary contemporaries.

Oliver Wendell Holmes died in 1894 at the age of eighty-six. He is known today for such works as "The Chambered Nautilus" and *Elsie Venner*. Much of his poetry and prose is ironic or satirical in nature, employing his sharp wit and clear-minded vision to call for change in society. But Dr. Holmes was a versatile man; just as he could conduct a medical career and achieve fame as a poet in the same lifetime, he could also balance the satiric wit of his lighter verse with the simple and reverent style of his religious verse. These poems, like all that he did in his lifetime, were expressions of his desire to serve his fellow man.

The Living Temple

O, Father!
grant Thy love divine
to make these mystic temples thine!

When wasting age
and wearying strife
have sapped the leaning walls of life,
when darkness gathers over all,
and the last tottering pillars fall,

take the poor dust
Thy mercy warms,
and mould it into heavenly forms!

Oliver Wendell Holmes

from The Chambered Nautilus

Build thee more stately mansions,
O my soul,
as the swift seasons roll!
Leave thy low-vaulted past!
Let each new temple,
nobler than the last,
shut thee from heaven
with a dome more vast,
till thou at length art free,
leaving thine outgrown shell
by life's unresting sea!

Oliver Wendell Holmes

Simple white frame churches like the Meeting House of the First Congregational Church in Williamstown, Massachusetts, are a common sight in the cities and towns of New England. The first Congregational churches in America were raised by Puritan settlers; they were named Congregational because their authority came not from a central ruling church, but from the members of the congregation. Oliver Wendall Holmes' father was a Congregational minister in Cambridge, Massachusetts, at the turn of the nineteenth century.

Lives of Private Devotion

"*O come, let us worship and bow down: let us kneel before the Lord our maker.*"

Psalm 95:6

College and university chapels provide students a place for common worship and solitary contemplation. This beautiful chapel is found on the campus of Rhodes College in Memphis, Tennessee.

Gerard Manley Hopkins

For many years students of English literature studied Gerard Manley Hopkins as a twentieth-century poet, despite the fact that he died before the end of the nineteenth century. In his lifetime, Hopkins' verses were circulated only among a small circle of his friends. At his death, they were bequeathed to a fellow poet for later publication. It was twenty-nine years after Hopkins' death before the first poem was published.

Hopkins was born in 1844 into a comfortable family in London and raised in the Church of England. While studying at Oxford University, he came under the influence of Catholic professors and tutors. In 1866, Hopkins converted to Roman Catholicism. As a result, he became estranged from his family. Eleven years later he entered the Society of Jesus. As a Jesuit, Hopkins served as parish priest and teacher throughout England, Wales, and Ireland.

Hopkins had been writing poetry since his days at Oxford; but before taking his religious vows, he burned all his poems, believing that poetry was irreconcilable with a life of faith. Throughout the remainder of his life, Hopkins struggled with his poetic talent and his concept of religious life. He finally returned to writing poetry only after his religious superiors urged him to use his God-given talent. He continued writing until his death in 1889.

Hopkins was keenly aware of the natural beauty of the world around him, and it gave him pleasure as an expression of the Divine. Although his poetry was written to glorify God's creation, he was never entirely comfortable with the poems, perhaps because he worried that he was also glorifying his own talent. But Hopkins had a wonderful and special gift. The combination of expressive language, unconventional rhythm, and the wild celebration of God's beauty produced poetry with an exuberance of spirit that belongs to the present as much as to the Victorian era in which it was written. Hopkins' poetry continues to glorify God and His creation to each generation.

God's Grandeur

The world is charged with the grandeur of God.
It will flame out, like shining from shook foil;
It gathers to a greatness, like the ooze of oil
Crushed.Why do men then now
not reck His rod?
Generations have trod, have trod, have trod;
And all is seared with trade; bleared,
smeared with toil;
And wears man's smudge and shares
man's smell: the soil
Is bare now, nor can foot feel,
being shod.

And for all this, nature is never spent;
There lives the dearest freshness
deep down things;
And though the last lights off the
black West went
Oh, morning, at the brown brink eastward, springs—
Because the Holy Ghost over the bent
World broods with warm breast
and with ah! bright wings.

Gerard Manley Hopkins

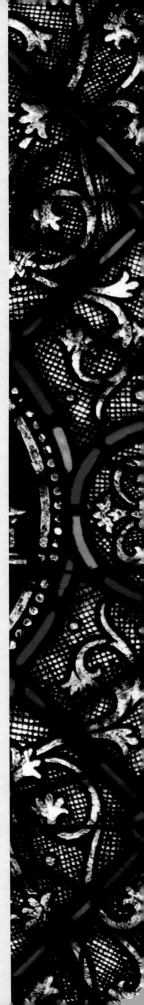

Pied Beauty

Glory be to God
for dappled things—
For skies of couple-color
as a brinded cow;

For rose-moles all in stipple
upon trout that swim;
Fresh-firecoal chestnut-falls,
finches' wings;

Landscape plotted and pierced—
fold, fallow, and plough;
And all trades,
their gear and tackle and trim.

All things counter,
original, spare, or strange;
Whatever is fickle,
freckled (who knows how?)

With swift, slow; sweet, sour; adazzle, dim;
He fathers-forth
whose beauty is past change:
Praise Him.

Gerard Manley Hopkins

After entering the Society of Jesus in 1877, Gerard Manley Hopkins spent his remaining years traveling the British countryside serving as a parish priest in small village churches like this one. In the peaceful countryside of England, Wales, and Ireland, Hopkins was able to serve God and also to indulge himself every day in the beauty of the natural world that inspired much of his poetry.

Anne Bradstreet

Anne Bradstreet, the first American poet, was born in England in 1612. She immigrated to America in 1630 as one of the first settlers of Massachusetts Bay Colony. At the time of her death in 1672, she had earned a reputation as a poet of considerable skill and a woman of great courage. Six years later in 1678 a volume of her poetry, *Several Poems Compiled by a Gentlewoman of New England*, was published in Boston. This volume, containing personal poems about her husband, her children, and the hardships of colonial life, earned Anne Bradstreet the reputation as America's first great poet.

Anne Bradstreet was eighteen when she left a comfortable home in England for the uncertainty of life in Massachusetts. At a time when daughters were rarely educated beyond domestic matters and the arts, Thomas Dudley tutored his daughter extensively in history, philosophy, and literature. At sixteen, Anne married Simon Bradstreet, a man who possessed qualities much like her father's. Her life in England was peaceful and fulfilling, but she crossed the sea to America to fulfill her duties to her husband and father—two men destined to play prominent roles in the government of the new Puritan colony.

Life in the colony was hard: the land was rugged, the winters were long, and provisions were scarce. There was little time for self-pity. Slowly, Anne Bradstreet began to accept her new home; eventually, she came to cherish it. She learned to love the rocky coastline, the silent, dark forests, and the deep winter snows. Bradstreet discovered that she was more than simply the wife and daughter who had obediently followed her husband and father; she was a strong and independent woman able to make a home for herself and her family under the most difficult circumstances. She learned that the faith that had inspired her husband and father to cross the Atlantic was equally strong in her, giving her the strength to face hardship and joy with the same stable heart.

Fame was never Anne Bradstreet's intention. Her poetry was written as an expression of the faith in God's guidance that gave meaning and purpose to her life. The faith of this woman tested by great hardship is a reminder that only by letting go of the things of this world and surrendering ourselves to God's guidance can we know the true depth of His love.

from Upon the Burning of My House

In silent night when rest I took,
For sorrow near I did not look,
I wakened was with thundering noise
And piteous shrieks of dreadful voice.
That fearful sound of fire and fire,
Let no man know, is my desire.

I, starting up, the light did spy.
And to my God my heart did cry
To strengthen me in my distress
And not to leave me succorless.
Then coming out beheld a space,
The flame consume my dwelling place. . . .

Here stood that trunk, and there that chest;
There lay that store I counted best:
My pleasant things in ashes lie,
And them behold no more shall I.
Under this roof no guest shall sit,
Nor at this table eat a bit.

Then straight I began my heart to chide,
And did thy wealth on earth abide?
Didst fix thy hope on mouldering dust,
The arm of flesh did make thy trust?
Raise up thy thoughts above the sky
That dunghill mists away may fly.

Thou hast a house on high erect,
Framed by that Mighty Architect,
With glory richly furnished,
Stands permanent though this be fled.
It is purchased and paid for too
By Him who has enough to do.

Anne Bradstreet

Lord, Why Should I Doubt?

Lord, why should I doubt anymore,
when You have given me such assured pledges of Your love?
First, You are my creator, I Your creature,
You my master, I Your servant.

But hence arises not my comfort: You are my Father, I Your child.
"You shall be my sons and daughters," says the Lord almighty.
Christ is my brother: "I ascend to my Father and your Father,
to my God and your God;
but, lest this should not be enough, your maker is your husband."

Nay, more, I am a member of His body, He my head.
Such privileges—had not the Word of truth made them known,
who or where is the man that dared in his heart have
presumed to have thought it? So wonderful are these thoughts
that my spirit fails in me at their consideration, and I am
confounded to think that God, who has done so much
for me, should have so little from me.

But this is my comfort, that when I come to heaven,
I shall understand perfectly what He has done for me,
and then I shall be able to praise Him as I ought.

Lord, having this hope, let me purify myself as You are pure,
and let me be no more afraid of death, but even desire to be
dissolved and be with You, which is best of all.

Anne Bradstreet

The Old Ship's Church in Hingham, Massachusetts, has been in continuous use since 1681. Hingham, a coastal town eleven miles south of Boston, was settled in 1633 as part of the same Massachusetts Bay Colony that brought Anne Bradstreet, her husband, and her father across the Atlantic three years earlier.

Christina Rossetti

The British poet Christina Rossetti lived a solitary, often painful life. The daughter of an Italian expatriate, Christina and her brothers and sister grew up in London. Their father, Gabriele Rossetti, painted and wrote poetry. His children seemed to inherit his artistic tendencies. Christina's older sister, Maria Francesca, was an author before entering an Anglican sisterhood, and her brothers, Dante Gabriel and William Michael, were both artists, art critics, and writers. As the youngest of the four children, Christina could not help but be a writer.

Much of Christina's youth was devoted to faithfully caring for her aging mother and father and to working with her older brothers and sister. Unfortunately, Christina could never replace the strong family ties of her youth. Twice, Christina's faith in God forced her to end engagements with men she thought she loved. In the first instance, her intended husband converted to Roman Catholicism and could no longer share her own Anglican faith. In the second case, the man she loved showed no interest at all in the spiritual life that was so vital to her.

Much of Rossetti's poetry is about the pain and frustration of her failed engagements and her struggles with loneliness. Her life, however, was not without joy. Although her verses about failed worldly loves often seem dark, her religious poetry is full of the joy of Christian faith. Christina Rossetti believed in the power of God to raise her above worldly concerns and problems. This faith bolstered her throughout her life.

The lines of Rossetti's religious poems and prayers speak directly to God. She does not ask for special favors but asks instead for the privilege of serving God on earth and eventually joining Him in heaven. Christina Rossetti sacrificed the opportunities for a husband and family of her own because her devotion to God was the most powerful and meaningful force in her life. The acceptance and hope expressed in her religious poetry attest to the fact that, although she felt the pain of the sacrifice, she never regretted her decisions. She was always able to find comfort in her faith.

Dost Thou Not Care?

I love and love not;
Lord it breaks my heart to love and not to love.
Thus veiled within Thy glory,
gone apart into Thy shrine, which is above.
Dost Thou not love me, Lord,
or care for this mine ill?

I love thee here or there,
I will accept thy broken heart; lie still.

Lord it was well with me in time gone by,
that cometh not again,
when I was fresh and cheerful;
worn with pain
now, out of sight and out of heart;
O, Lord, how long?

I watch thee as thou art;
I will accept thy fainting heart; be strong.

"Lie still," "be strong," today;
but, Lord, tomorrow, what of tomorrow, Lord?
Shall there be rest from toil, be truce from sorrow,
be living green upon the sward
now but a barren grave to me,
be joy or sorrow?

Did I not die for thee? Do I not live for thee?
Leave me tomorrow.

Christina Rossetti

Uphill

Does the road wind uphill all the way?
Yes, to the very end.
Will the day's journey take the whole long day?
From morn to night, my friend.

But is there for the night a resting place?
A roof for when the slow dark hours begin.
May not the darkness hide it from my face?
You cannot miss that inn.

Shall I meet other wayfarers at night?
Those who have gone before.
Then must I knock, or call when just in sight?
They will not keep you standing at the door.

Shall I find comfort, travel-sore and weak?
Of labor you shall find the sum.
Will there be beds for me and all who seek?
Yea, beds for all who come.

Christina Rossetti

Like the women at the tomb portrayed in this stained glass from St. Mary's and St. Joseph's Church in Bedale, England, Christina Rossetti gave herself entirely to Christ. Her poems and the example of her life express a love for Christ strong enough to transcend all the disappointments and temptations of the world and lead her to peace.

Alice Cary

Alice Cary was one of the most popular American poets of the mid-nineteenth century. Her simple and sincere verses appeared regularly in journals and newspapers across the country, and she was befriended and praised by such literary greats as John Greenleaf Whittier and Edgar Allan Poe. Today, more than one hundred years after her death, the lovely verses of this simple Ohio farm girl still hold the power to comfort and inspire.

Alice Cary was born in 1820 in Hamilton County, Ohio, the fourth of Robert and Elizabeth Cary's nine children. She grew up on an isolated farm in an atmosphere of hard work, frugality, and close family ties. The Cary children attended school occasionally, but most of their education took place on the farm. Alice learned to read from the Bible; there were few other books available to her. Nonetheless, she and a younger sister, Phoebe, developed a love for poetry and began to compose their own verses. In 1838, Alice's love for poetry became a career when one of her poems was accepted for publication in a Cincinnati newspaper.

The Cincinnati publication led to others in the area, some of which caught the eye of Washington, D.C., publisher Gamaliel Bailey. In 1847, Bailey published a series of Alice's poetry in the *National Era*. These poems inspired the interest of Whittier and Poe, whose praise convinced Rufus Griswold to include Alice in his popular anthology, *The Female Poets of America*. In 1850, Griswold also published *The Poems of Alice and Phoebe Cary*, which sealed Alice's place among the most widely read poets of the day.

After the appearance of their book, the Cary sisters moved to New York to devote themselves fully to their literary careers. Alice was the more prolific writer of the sisters. In addition to her poetry, she wrote a series of short stories about life in rural Ohio. She continued to publish her work in journals and newspapers until her death in 1871 at the age of fifty.

Even in her years in New York City, Alice Cary never strayed from the roots of her Ohio childhood. As a girl, she learned that family and faith are the pillars of life; her verses are a testament to the fact that nothing she encountered away from the farm persuaded her otherwise.

A Prayer

I have been little used to frame
Wishes to speech and call it prayer;
Today, my Father, in Thy name,
I ask to have my soul stripped bare
Of all its vain pretense,—to see
Myself, as I am seen by Thee.

I want to know how much the pain
And passion here, its powers abate;
To take its thoughts, a tangled skein,
And stretch them out all smooth and straight;
To track its wavering course through sin
And sorrow, to its origin.

I want to know if in the night
Of evil, grace doth so abound,
That from its darkness we draw light,
As flowers do beauty from the ground:
Or, if the sins of time shall be
The shadows of eternity.

I want, though only for an hour,
To be myself,—to get more near
The wondrous mystery and power
Of love, whose echoes floating here,
Between us and the waiting grave,
Make all of light, of heaven, we have.
Amen.

Alice Cary

Supplication

O Thou, who all my life hast crowned
With better things than I could ask,
Be it today my humble task
To own from depths of grief profound,
The many sins, which darken through
    What little good I do.

I have been too much used, I own,
To tell my need in fretful words;
The clamoring of the silly birds,
Impatient till their wings be grown,
Have Thy forgiveness, O my blessed Lord,
    The like to me accord.

Of grace, as much as will complete
Thy will in me, I pray Thee for;
Even as a rose shut in a drawer
That maketh all about it sweet,
I would be, rather than the cedar fine;
    Help me Thou Power divine.

With charity fill Thou my heart,
As summer fills the grass with dews,
And as the year itself renews
In the sun when winter days depart,
Blessed Forever, grant Thou me
    To be renewed in Thee.
    Amen.

Alice Cary

St. Patrick's Cathedral is one of the most beautiful churches in New York City, where Alice Cary and her sister made their home for almost twenty years. Although the sisters never lost touch with their Ohio farm roots, they became prominent figures in New York, hosting Sunday evening receptions in their home attended by the leading literary and cultural figures of the day.

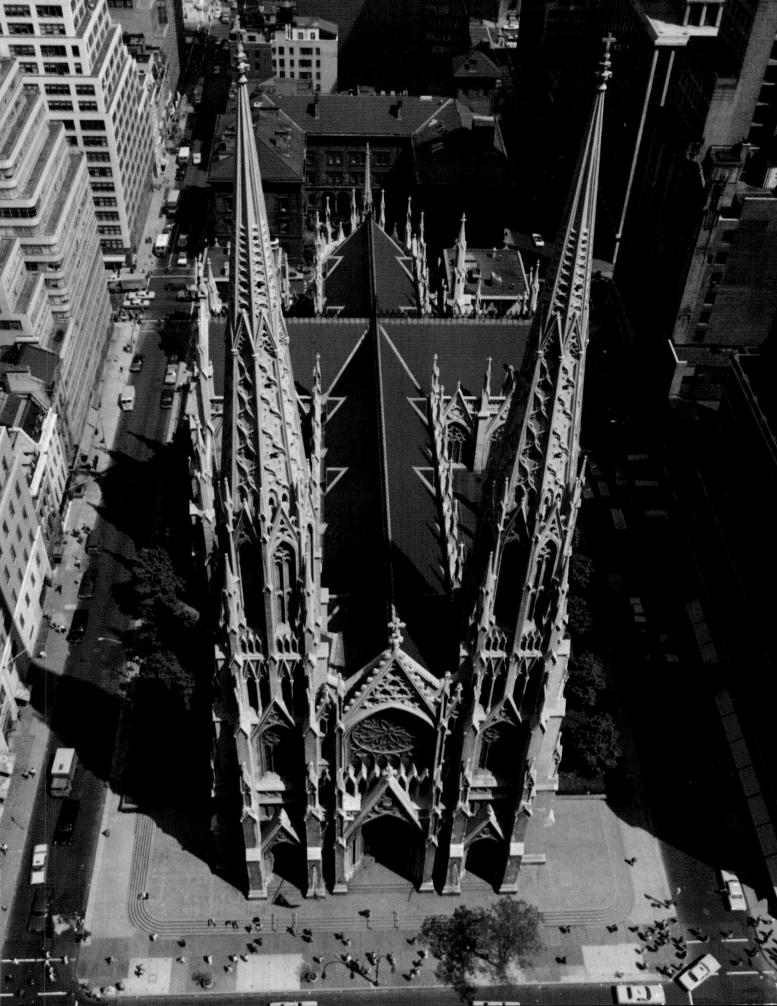

Thomas Merton

Throughout his entire life, Thomas Merton enjoyed the excitement of new experiences and challenges. He was born in 1915 in France, to an American mother and New Zealand father, both of whom were artists. Merton was educated at Cambridge in England, and Columbia in New York City. As a young college student, he was attractive, outgoing, and popular, and he found it easy to indulge himself in the pleasures of the world. The world, however, left Merton dissatisfied. While in his twenties, at Columbia University, Thomas Merton began the search for meaning in his life. His search brought him to the Catholic church, where he found the meaning that had eluded him.

At the age of twenty-six, Merton took the vows of a Trappist monk. He joined the silent life of an order that believes the elimination of the world's distractions frees the mind for deeper religious contemplation. In the peaceful world of a Kentucky monastery, he wrote his spiritual biography, *The Seven Storey Mountain*, and sixty books of poetry, essays, and history.

Except for brief trips outside, Merton remained at the monastery until his death in 1968. His work's impact, however, was not limited to inside the monastery's walls. In the 1960s, he wrote about the problem of civil rights and the threat of nuclear war in the United States. Through his writings, he touched an entire generation and proved that religious thought can connect man to the world.

Even after recognizing God as the path to peace and satisfaction, Merton did not stop searching for the unclouded understanding that is attainable only through a life guided by faith. Merton's life and writings prove that when he surrendered to God's guidance, he better understood the world and could better serve man. And in serving others, he was serving God.

The Road Ahead

My Lord, God,
I have no idea where I am going.
I do not see the road ahead of me.
I cannot know for certain where it will end.
Nor do I really know myself,
and the fact that I think I am following
Your will does not mean that I am actually doing so.
But I believe that the desire to please You
does in fact please You.
And I hope I have that desire in all that I am doing.

I hope that I will never do anything
apart from that desire.
And I know that if I do this,
You will lead me by the right road,
though I may know nothing about it.
Therefore will I trust You always
though I may seem to be lost
in the shadow of death.
I will not fear for You are ever with me,
and You will never leave me to face my perils alone.

Thomas Merton

We Give Thee Thanks

We give Thee thanks, O God,
for great moments of joy and strength
that come to us when by a strong
and special movement of grace
we are able to perform some act of pure
and disinterested love.

For the clean fire of that love
which floods the soul and cleanses
the whole man and leaves us filled with
an unexpected lightness and freedom for action.

For the moment of pure prayer
which not only establishes order in the soul,
but even fortifies us against physical weariness
and brings us a new lease on life itself.
Glory be to Thee
for Thy precious gift!

Thomas Merton

Pictured at left are the cloisters at Wells Cathedral in
Wells, England. The twelfth-century church is England's
oldest Gothic cathedral, and the only one not located
within a major city. The peace and seclusion of Wells is
reminiscent of the life-transforming retreat Thomas Merton found at the Trappist monastery.

Lives of Public Testimony

"How beautiful
upon the mountains
are the feet
of him that
bringeth
good tidings. . . ."

Isaiah 52:7

American churches are found wherever people settled and
discovered that they needed a place to seek God and pray.
The Chapel of the Transfiguration Episcopal Church, in
the rugged mountains of the American West, is proof that
man's need to pray follows him wherever he goes.

Phillips Brooks

While achieving fame in the world's eyes, Phillips Brooks led a life devoted to God. A theology graduate from Harvard in 1855, Brooks ministered to two large congregations, first at Holy Trinity Church in Philadelphia and later at Trinity Church in Boston. Before his death in 1893 at fifty-eight, he became Bishop of Massachusetts. Yet for all his honors and worldly achievements, Brooks is best remembered as the author of one of our most beloved Christmas carols, "O Little Town of Bethlehem."

Brooks, while a rector at Holy Trinity in Philadelphia, traveled to the Holy Land for a year. During this time, he retraced the steps of Jesus and the Apostles. On Christmas Eve, he attended the service in the ancient Basilica of Constantine in Bethlehem. The experience was an emotional one for Brooks and would remain with him throughout his life.

Once back in Philadelphia, Brooks wrote "O Little Town of Bethlehem." The hymn is the simple yet moving expression of the joy of Jesus' birth and the "wondrous gift" of God's love, accessible to all people young and old. In the words of this hymn, Brooks demonstrated his greatest talent: the ability to express the most complex religious doctrine in a simple, understandable way, not by making it less important, but by making it less intimidating. Brooks' Christianity was positive and celebratory, and his enthusiasm was contagious.

When asked to accept the position of Bishop of Massachusetts, Brooks hesitated only because he feared that he would lose touch with the people he meant to serve. When he assumed the post, however, he continued his devoted service to his congregation and spread his love and faith even further than he could have as pastor of any single church. Through his carol "O Little Town of Bethlehem," he spread his message to the world.

O Little Town of Bethlehem

O little town of Bethlehem,
how still we see thee lie!
Above thy deep and dreamless sleep
the silent stars go by;

Yet in thy dark streets shineth
the everlasting light;
The hopes and fears of all the years
are met in thee tonight.

For Christ is born of Mary,
and gathered all above,
While mortals sleep, the angels keep
their watch of wond'ring love.

O morning stars, together
proclaim the holy birth,
And praises sing to God the King,
and peace to men on earth.

O holy Child of Bethlehem!
Descend to us, we pray.
Cast out our sin, and enter in,
be born in us today!

We hear the Christmas angels,
the great glad tidings tell;
O come to us, abide with us,
our Lord Immanuel!

Phillips Brooks

A Prayer

O Lord,
by all Your dealings with us,
whether of joy or pain,
of light or darkness,
let us be brought to You.
Let us value no treatment of Your grace
simply because it makes us happy
or because it makes us sad,
because it gives us or denies us what we want;
but may all that You send us bring us to You;
that knowing Your perfectness,
we may be sure in every disappointment
You are still loving us,
in every darkness
You are still enlightening us,
and in every enforced idleness
You are giving us life,
as in His death
You gave life to Your Son,
our Saviour,
Jesus Christ.
Amen.

Phillips Brooks

This stained glass window is one of many inside Trinity Church, one of the most beautiful landmarks in the city of Boston, Massachusetts. Outside Trinity Church stands a memorial to one of its greatest and most beloved ministers, Phillips Brooks. The statue, completed in 1907 by American sculptor Augustus Saint-Gaudens, commemorates Phillips Brooks' years of faithful service to the Trinity congregation.

St. Anselm

Anselm, Benedictine theologian, archbishop of Canterbury, and Christian saint, was born in 1033 in the village of Aosta in Piedmont, northern Italy. His father was a wealthy landowner, and he provided his son with an excellent education. His father was also a stubborn and domineering man unwilling to let his bright young son make his own decisions. When Anselm, at fifteen, declared that he would enter a monastery and devote his life to God, his father vehemently objected, and young Anselm was forced to delay his plans.

Anselm, however, was as stubborn in his convictions as his father was in his objections. He obeyed his father for several years, but he never abandoned his plans for a religious life. In 1056, following the death of his mother, Anselm crossed the Alps into Normandy, where he joined a monastic school. At the monastery, Anselm quickly earned a reputation as an enlightened and gentle man. The older monks found Anselm always ready for a conversation or debate and always able to explain his beliefs or actions with compelling, rational arguments. This quality served Anselm well later in life when he traveled to England to serve as archbishop of Canterbury. In this post, Anselm maintained his religious convictions in the face of great political pressure from two kings, William Rufus and Henry I, who were more interested in their own sovereignty than that of God. Anselm's calm reasoning is also the reason his volumes of writing on religious questions have been so widely read; Anselm's faith was emotional, but he was able to justify his faith in a way so concrete and rational that it was compelling to believers and non-believers alike.

Much of Anselm's writing consists of treatises on the great questions of religion: Does God exist? Why did God send His Son to earth to redeem man? Anselm answers each question in a logical, structured manner, eliminating doubt by eliminating argument. But his prayers reveal a more gentle, emotional side of his faith. Anselm found peace in the religious life and in his close relationship with God; it is this peace that is reflected in the words of his prayers.

We Love You, O God

We love You, O God;
and we desire to love You more and more.
Grant us that we may love You as much as we desire,
and as much as we ought.

O dearest Friend, who has so loved and saved us,
the thought of whom is so sweet
and always growing sweeter,
come with Christ and dwell in our hearts;
then You will keep a watch over our lips,
our steps, our deeds, and we shall not need
to be anxious either for our souls or our bodies.
Give us love, sweetest of all gifts,
which knows no enemy.

Give us in our hearts pure love,
born of Your love to us,
that we may love others as You love us.

O most loving Father of Jesus Christ,
from whom flows all love,
let our hearts, frozen in sin,
cold to You and cold to others,
be warmed by this divine fire.
So help and bless us in Your Son.
Amen.

St. Anselm

A Call to Meditation

Come now, little man,
turn aside for a while from
your daily employment,
escape for a moment from
the tumult of your thoughts.

Cast aside your weighty cares,
let your burdensome distractions wait,
free yourself awhile for God
and rest awhile in Him.

Enter the inner chamber of your soul,
shut out everything except God
and that which can help you in seeking Him,
and when you have shut the door, seek Him.

Now, my whole heart, say to God,
"I seek Your face,
Lord, it is Your face I seek."

St. Anselm

Since the beginning of British Christianity, Canterbury
Cathedral has been the center of English religious life. It is
best known as the seat of the head of the Church of England, the archbishop of Canterbury, and as the destination
of pilgrimages like the one described in Chaucer's *Canterbury Tales*. As archbishop of Canterbury, St. Anselm is
part of a tradition that goes back to the sixth century and
includes such memorable religious figures as Thomas à
Becket and Thomas Cranmer.

Jonathan Edwards

Jonathan Edwards was born in Connecticut in 1703. Educated at home by his minister father and his mother, the young Edwards was intelligent and very precocious. At the age of thirteen, he enrolled at Yale University. While at Yale, Edwards underwent a religious conversion which he described in his *Personal Narrative*. After graduation, Edwards briefly served as minister of a Presbyterian church in New York City before returning to Yale as a tutor. In 1727, he was appointed assistant pastor to his grandfather, Solomon Stoddard, a respected minister at Northampton, Massachusetts.

Edwards became a powerful preacher, one who frightened his congregation with visions of damnation but also inspired and comforted them with beautiful descriptions of God's grace. He sparked a revival of religious fervor known as the Great Awakening; but his authority did not last. Eventually Edwards was forced out of his position in the church by parishioners who objected to his strict standards for church membership. Edwards left Northampton to become minister at Stockbridge, Massachusetts, where he served until 1757. In that year, Edwards was elected president of Princeton University, an office he held until his death in 1758.

Jonathan Edwards was not obsessed with man's damnation. He was awed by the beauty of nature and pondered the greatness of its Creator. He could not, however, ignore the suffering in the world. Edwards dared ask, "Could the same God who made the earth and sky have created such hardship for His people?" In the midst of such turmoil, Edwards found the following words in Timothy: "Now unto the King eternal, immortal, invisible, the only wise God, be honor and glory for ever and ever."

Overcome by a certain understanding that God was perfect and wise, Edwards concluded that man's suffering was the result of man's defiance of God's original covenant. Edwards had glimpsed the beauty and power of God, and he labored his whole life to share this knowledge with others. The words of his prayers and sermons leave no doubt of his absolute faith in the sovereignty of God and the power of His grace.

from The Personal Narrative

It has often appeared to me delightful,
to be united to Christ,
to have Him for my head,
and to be a member of His body;
also to have Christ as my teacher and my prophet.
I very often think with sweetness, and longings,
and pantings of soul, of being a little child
taking hold of Christ,
to be led by Him through the wilderness of this world. . . .

I love to think of coming to Christ,
to receive salvation of Him,
poor in spirit and quite empty of self,
humbly exalting Him alone;
cut off entirely from my own root,
in order to grow into,
and out of Christ;
to have God in Christ to be all in all;
and to live by faith in the Son of God,
a life of humble, unfeigned confidence in Him.

Jonathan Edwards

The Beauty of Holiness

Holiness appeared to me
to be of a sweet, pleasant,
charming, serene, calm nature;
which brought an inexpressible
purity, brightness, peacefulness,
and ravishment to the soul.
In other words, that it made the soul
like a garden of God,
with all manner of pleasant flowers.

He that sees the beauty of holiness,
or true moral good,
sees the greatest and
most important thing in the world. . . .
Unless this is seen
nothing is seen that is worth seeing;
for there is no other true excellence or beauty.

Jonathan Edwards

It was late in his life, after a long and controversial career as a preacher, that Jonathan Edwards was elected president of Princeton University, then known as New Jersey College. Edwards served only five weeks before he died of complications following a smallpox inoculation. Today, almost two hundred and fifty years later, Princeton remains one of America's most distinguished universities. Pictured is the Princeton University Chapel.

Lottie Moon

From an early age, it was clear that Lottie Moon, the Southern Baptist missionary honored each year by the Lottie Moon Christmas Offering, was destined for something beyond an ordinary life. Christened Charlotte, Lottie was born in 1840 on Viewmont Plantation near Scottsville, Virginia. She was the third child in a very accomplished family. Her father was a successful merchant and planter, and her older sister Oriana was the first southern woman to earn a medical degree, graduating from the Female Medical College of Pennsylvania. Lottie seemed ready to follow in her older sister's footsteps. She earned her Bachelor of Arts degree from Valley Union Seminary and then became one of the first women in the South to receive a graduate degree, earning her Masters degree in 1861 from Albermarle Institute in Charlottesville.

Until a Baptist revival in Charlottesville in 1859, however, Lottie was all ambition and no direction. It was at this revival that Moon underwent a sudden conversion and devoted her life to God. After completing her studies at Albermarle, Moon returned home to the plantation to help her widowed mother through the Civil War years; but her eyes remained focused on God as she patiently awaited her opportunity to serve. That opportunity came in 1872, when the Southern Baptist church decided to allow women to serve in China as missionaries. Moon volunteered; from 1877 until her death, Lottie Moon lived in China, spreading the message of Christianity to Chinese women and girls. Her life was never easy. In addition to the difficulties of living in an undeveloped region thousands of miles from home, she met with opposition from her church, which discouraged her emphasis on teaching and converting women and girls. But Moon's response to discouragement was to work even harder. She founded the Women's Missionary Union and began an annual Christmas offering to raise money for women to pursue missionary work where they had previously been excluded.

Lottie Moon died in 1912 on a ship in a Japanese harbor. She was returning home at seventy-one years of age, suffering from near starvation after giving her salary to feed the Chinese victims of a famine. Her death mirrored the life she had lived for fifty-three years in China—one devoted to serving God before serving herself.

from a Letter

This ancient continent of Asia
whose soil you are treading
was the chosen theatre for the advent
of the Son of God.

In a rush of grateful emotion
there come to your mind
the lines of that grand old hymn
the *Dies Irae*,
"Seeking me
Thy worn feet hastened,
On the cross
Thy soul death tasted,"
and your heart is all aglow with longing
to bear to others the priceless gift
that you have received
that thus you may manifest
your thankfulness and love to the giver.

He "went about doing good;"
in a humble manner
you are trying to walk
in His footsteps.
As you wind your way
from village to village,
you feel it is no idle fancy
that the Master walks beside you
and you hear His voice
saying gently,
"Lo! I am with you always
even unto the end."

Lottie Moon

"GO YE THEREFORE AND TEACH ALL NATIONS."

MISS LOTTIE MOON
OUR BELOVED MISSIONARY
BORN DEC.12.1840 — DIED DEC.24.1912.

from a Letter

Is it any wonder
that as you draw near to the village
a feeling of exultation comes over you?

That your heart goes up to God
in glad thanksgiving
that He has so trusted you
as to commit to your hands this glorious gospel
that you may convey its blessings
to those who still sit in darkness?

When the heart is full of such joy
it is no effort to speak to the people;
you could not keep silent if you would.

Mere physical hardships
sink into . . . insignificance.
What does one care
for comfortless inns,
hard beds,
hard fare,
when all around
is a world of joy
and glory
and beauty?

Lottie Moon

This stained glass window at Crewe Baptist Church in Crewe, Virginia, pays tribute to one of the most remarkable and committed missionaries in Southern Baptist history. Lottie Moon not only brought Christianity to countless Chinese, she also paved the way for future generations of Christian women determined to serve God without limitation.

Peter Marshall

Peter Marshall was born in Coatsbridge, Scotland, in 1902. As a young man, he committed himself to God's service but found little opportunity in his native country. In 1927, he boarded a ship for America, believing that on the other side of the Atlantic he would find the means to answer God's call. In his adopted country, he became Chaplain of the Senate. In only two short years, Peter Marshall transformed what had previously been a ceremonial opening prayer into a sincere call for God's guidance and convinced a nation that God can and does act in the daily events and decisions of our lives.

Peter Marshall did not always want to become a minister. As a child he fell in love with the sea and wanted to join the British Navy. Fatherless from an early age, Marshall looked to the navy as his escape from a difficult home life. Circumstances, however, kept him away from the navy and left him a restless young man searching for direction. He found that direction in the service of God. After hearing a recruitment talk by a group of missionaries, Peter Marshall stood before the group and announced that from that day forward his life would be dedicated to his Lord. Marshall wanted to serve as a missionary in China, but the money to support such a mission did not exist. He resigned himself to service at home in Scotland, where he struggled for years without success to earn the money to study for the ministry. The suggestion of a cousin led Marshall to America.

From the moment Peter Marshall first stepped in front of an American congregation, his ministerial gift was apparent. He served congregations in Birmingham, Atlanta, and Washington, D.C., before his appointment as Chaplain of the United States Senate. His daily prayers to the senators were constant reminders that they were serving God as well as themselves and the people of their states. Marshall preached that God existed not just in history, but also in the immediate present. His sermons were delivered with the enthusiasm and sincerity of a true friend, and his words remain an inspiration to all Americans. When Peter Marshall died in 1949, his brief term as Senate Chaplain ended; but in the short time God allowed him, he left a lasting impression on his adopted homeland.

With Sorrow and True Repentance

Forgive me, Lord Jesus,
for the things that I have done that make
me feel uncomfortable in Thy presence.
All the front that I polish so carefully for men to see,
does not deceive Thee.

For Thou knowest every thought
that has left its shadow on my memory.
Thou hast marked every motive
that curdled something sweet within me.

I acknowledge, with sorrow and true repentance,
that I have desired that which I should not have;
I have toyed with what I knew was not for me;
I have been preoccupied with self-interest;
I have invited unclean thoughts into my mind
and entertained them as honored guests;
my ears have often been deaf to Thy whisper;
my eyes have often been blind to the signs of Thy guidance.
Make me willing to be changed,
even though it requires surgery of the soul,
and therapy of discipline.

Make my heart warm and soft, that I may receive
and accept now the blessing of Thy forgiveness,
the benediction of
Thy "Depart in peace . . . and sin no more."
In Jesus' name.
Amen.

Peter Marshall

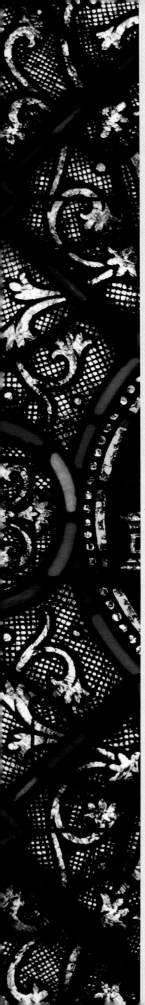

Charles Wesley

Charles Wesley, born in 1708 in Lincolnshire, England, was the eighteenth child born to Samuel and Susanna Wesley. Charles lived much of his life in the shadow of his older brother John, the founder of the Methodist church. Like all nine of the surviving Wesley children, Charles benefitted from a thorough and strict early education. He followed brother John to Oxford, and it was Charles who founded the Holy Club which John shaped into the forerunner of Methodism. After Oxford, Charles followed his brother once more, this time to the colony of Georgia, where both hoped to serve as missionaries.

In Georgia, Charles found his existence miserable; the colonists were not interested in his preaching. Charles returned to England in the midst of a personal spiritual crisis. Through discussions with a Moravian, Charles learned that he needed a deep, personal reliance upon Christ. Without such dependence, the practices of his religious rituals and disciplines were empty.

When John Wesley set out to spread the message of Methodism to the English people, Charles was ready to follow him. The brothers rode side by side for nearly fifty years, spreading the message of salvation through faith. Their newfound faith found unique expression within each of them. John Wesley's legacy lies in the form and foundation of the Methodist church, while Charles Wesley became the most prolific writer of hymns in world history.

Charles Wesley began writing poetry and hymns at an early age. His mother, however, discouraged his creative efforts due to her fear that they would divert him from the pursuit of a serious religious life. But Charles Wesley's faith expressed itself naturally in words and music. He wrote wherever he was, even on horseback as he traveled from one remote country village to another. His hymns helped bring Methodism to the common English people, who were unlikely to be impressed by doctrine but quick to embrace the words of an uplifting hymn.

Charles' hymns are evidence that true faith will find a different expression in every individual; what is important is not the form faith takes but the depth of its roots in the heart of the believer. Charles Wesley left more than 6,500 hymns to attest to the depth of his own faith.

The Incarnation

Glory be to God on high,
And peace on earth descend:
God comes down: He bows the Sky:
He shows himself our Friend!
God the invisible appears,
God the blest, the Great I Am
Sojourns in His vale of tears.
And Jesus is the name.

Him the angels all adored
Their maker and their king:
Tidings of their humbled lord
They now to mortals bring:
Emptied of His majesty,
Of His dazzling glories shorn,
Being's source begins to be
And God Himself is born!

See the eternal Son of God
A mortal son of man,
Dwelling in an earthly clod
Whom Heaven cannot contain!
Stand amazed, ye Heavens at this!
See the Lord of Earth and Skies
Humbled to the dust He is,
And in a manger lies!

We the Sons of Men rejoice,
The Prince of Peace proclaim,
With Heaven's Host lift up our voice,
And shout Immanuel's name;
Knees and hearts to Him we bow;
Of our flesh and of our bone
Jesus is our brother now,
And God is all our own!

Charles Wesley

Love Divine, All Loves Excelling

Love Divine, all loves excelling,
Joy of heaven, to earth come down,
Fix in us Thy humble dwelling,
All Thy faithful mercies crown.
Jesus, Thou art all compassion,
Pure unbounded love Thou art;
Visit us in Thy salvation,
Enter every trembling heart.

Breathe, O breathe Thy loving spirit
Into every troubled breast;
Let us all in Thee inherit,
Let us find that second rest:
Take away our power of sinning,
Alpha and Omega be,
End of faith as its beginning,
Set our hearts at liberty.

Finish then Thy new Creation,
Pure and spotless let us be;
Let us see Thy great salvation
Perfectly restored in Thee,
Changed from glory into glory
Till in heaven we take our place,
Till we cast our crowns before Thee,
Lost in wonder, love, and praise!

Charles Wesley

The organ once played by Charles Wesley is preserved in
the Foundry Chapel, a side chapel to the Wesley Chapel
in London, England. The chapel, pictured at left is visited
by thousands of visitors each year, most of whom have at
one time or another sung one of Wesley's hymns.

John Greenleaf Whittier

For many students, John Greenleaf Whittier is the poetical voice of nineteenth-century America. The son of a poor farmer, he was largely self-educated, but his poems "Barbara Freitchie" and "Barefoot Boy" have made him recognizable, if not unforgettable. During the mid-1800s, however, Whittier's writing was not confined to poetry. As an editor for a Boston weekly, his essays promoted abolition and pacifism, causes which, although contrary at the time, are consistent with his Quaker faith.

Born in 1807 on a farm near Haverhill, Massachusetts, Whittier lived during rising political tensions and the Civil War. As a Quaker, he never doubted where his sympathies lay; he could not believe in the enslavement of another human being for any reason. Whittier, however, was not only an abolitionist; he was a pacifist and could not support a war even for the purpose of freedom from slavery.

At the height of the conflict, Whittier was a prominent and highly respected newspaper editor whose gentle faith spoke in a fervent voice. Consequently, he became an influential advocate of both causes. For the greater part of his life, he continued to use his skills and influence to promote the abolition of slavery and the maintenance of peace. His prose works, such as *The Voices of Freedom* and *In War Time and Other Poems*, advanced the cause of reform and helped re-elect President Lincoln.

At the end of the Civil War, Whittier turned his energies and talents to poetry. His subjects became the rural life and customs of New England, captured in poems such as "Snow-Bound" and "Sundown." These gentle works came from the same man who had worked so unceasingly and vigorously for the causes of abolition and pacifism. In his later poems as in his earlier essays, Whittier continued to advocate responsibility for one's fellowman. His message celebrated God's power and guidance but also acknowledged man's obligation on earth to live in kindness and love.

A Prayer

Let the lowliest task be mine,
Grateful, so the work be Thine;
Let me find the humblest place
In the shadow of Thy grace;
Blest to me were any spot
Where temptation whispers not.
If there be some weaker one,
Give me strength to help him on;
If a blinder soul there be,
Let me guide him nearer Thee.

Make my mortal dreams come true
With the work I fain would do;
Clothe with life the weak intent,
Let me be the thing I meant;
Let me find in Thy employ
Peace that dearer is than joy.
Out of self to love be led,
And to heaven acclimated,
Until all things sweet and good
Seem my natural habitude.

John Greenleaf Whittier

Andrew Rykman's Prayer

Pardon, Lord, the lips that dare
Shape in words a mortal's prayer!
Prayer, that, when my day is done,
And I see its setting sun,
Shorn and beamless, cold and dim,
Sink beneath the horizon's rim,—

When this ball of rock and clay
Crumbles from my feet away,
And the solid shores of sense
Melt into the vague immense,
Father! I may come to Thee
Even with the beggar's plea,
As the poorest of Thy poor,
With my needs and nothing more . . . .

John Greenleaf Whittier

This Quaker church in Wenham, Massachusetts, is probably not much different than the one John Greenleaf Whittier attended in his hometown of Haverhill, a few miles to the northwest. The Quakers, also known as the Religious Society of Friends, were begun in England in 1652 by George Fox, who believed that there "was that of God in every man," and that by following that presence of the Divine within himself, each man could live a righteous life. Quaker worship consists of group meetings at which all members are welcome to speak.

Isaac Watts

Isaac Watts, the man responsible for such beloved hymns as *Joy to the World* and *When I Survey the Wondrous Cross*, was born on July 17, 1674, in Southampton, England. His first attempt at writing hymns was in response to a challenge from his father. Isaac, a precocious fifteen-year-old who could read and write in several languages and who had a habit of conversing in rhyme, had complained that the hymns recited each week at Sunday service were putting the congregation to sleep rather than inspiring them to more meaningful worship. The senior Watts told his son to either stop complaining or provide the congregation with something better. Within a week Isaac had done just that, taking a popular psalm and turning it into poetry. On the following Sunday, his newly arranged hymn was presented to the congregation. Isaac had found his gift; his songs inspired his fellow worshippers and brought new life to the service.

For the next ten years, Isaac Watts continued to write hymns while he studied for the ministry. At first he simply paraphrased the psalms, giving poetic form to the words. Later as he matured, he composed original poetry to be set to music. In total, Watts wrote almost six hundred hymns, many of which are still sung today. By the age of twenty-five, however, Watts had all but given up hymn writing in favor of preaching and theological writing. For over a decade, Watts was a popular preacher in London. After 1712, because of ill health, he gave up full-time preaching and devoted his time to writing.

Many of Watts' theological treatises and essays were required reading at Cambridge, Oxford, Yale, and Harvard until the early nineteenth century. A man of great intelligence with impeccable powers of reason, he was also a man who fully embraced the mystery of God and power of true faith. Isaac Watts died in 1748 at the age of seventy-four. In his long life, he used his gift of language to provide the academic world with volumes of theology and to bless Christians everywhere with inspirational hymns.

A Prospect of Heaven

There is a land of pure delight
Where saints immortal reign;
Infinite day excludes the night,
And pleasures banish pain.

There everlasting spring abides,
And never-withering flowers:
Death like a narrow sea divides
This heavenly land from ours.

Sweet field beyond the swelling flood
Stand dressed in living green:
So to the Jews old Canaan stood,
While Jordan rolled between.

But timorous mortals start and shrink
To cross this narrow sea,
And linger shivering on the brink
And fear to launch away.

O could we make our doubts remove,
These gloomy doubts that rise,
And see the Canaan that we love
With unbeclouded eyes,

Could we but climb where Moses stood,
And view the landscape o'er,
Not Jordan's stream, nor Death's cold flood,
Should fright us from the shore.

Isaac Watts

When I Survey the Wondrous Cross

When I survey the wondrous Cross
Where the young Prince of Glory died,
My richest gain I count but loss,
And pour contempt on all my pride.

Forbid it, Lord, that I should boast
Save in the death of Christ, my God;
All the vain things that charm me most,
I sacrifice them to His blood.

See from His head, His hands, His feet,
Sorrow and love flow mingled down;
Did e'er such love and sorrow meet?
Or thorns compose so rich a crown?

His dying crimson like a robe
Spreads o'er His body on the Tree,
Then am I dead to all the globe,
And all the globe is dead to me.

Were the whole realm of nature mine,
That were a present far too small;
Love so amazing, so divine,
Demands my soul, my life, my all.

Isaac Watts

Throughout Christian history, artists have used their work to inspire others to greater faith. This awesome stained glass window in St. Catherine Cree in London creates a mood of reverence in those who worship beneath it, just as Isaac Watts' hymns enrich with their joyous praise the worship of the congregations who sing them.

George Macdonald

George Macdonald was born in Huntly, Aberdeenshire, Scotland, in 1824. From childhood, his education was aimed at the ministry. As a young man he studied at King's College, Aberdeen University and later at Highbury College in London. He became a Congregational minister in 1850 and was assigned to preach at Arundel in Sussex. Poor health, however, altered Macdonald's plans for a life of holy service. After only three years as a minister, his failing health forced him to find a quieter life's work.

In 1850, Macdonald turned to writing as both his career and an alternate means of serving God. He moved first to Manchester, England, and shortly thereafter to London. He devoted himself to poetry, children's stories, and novels. His publications span almost forty years; his first piece was a dramatic poem published in 1855, and his final work was a two-volume set of his own poetry compiled in 1893. His best-known novels, *David Elginbrod* and *Robert Falconer*, are stories of life in the Scottish countryside. His best-known children's story, *At the Back of the North Wind*, was published in 1871.

George Macdonald died in 1905 in England at the age of eighty. His most lasting work remains his poetry, which still appears in anthologies of religious verse and prayer. Macdonald had a very simple understanding of his relationship with God: God was the father and George Macdonald the child. He did not question the sudden and premature end to his career as a minister; he simply found another way to serve. George Macdonald fully accepted his own dependence upon God's leadership. His philosophy is summed up by the last lines of one of his poems in which he gives himself to God: "Besmirched and ragged, Lord, take back thine own: A fool I bring thee to be made a child."

Hunger for Righteousness

Father, I cry to Thee for bread,
With hungered longing, eager prayer;
Thou hear'st and givest me instead
More hunger and a half despair.

O Lord! how long? My days decline,
My youth is lapped in memories old,
I need not bread alone, but wine—
See, cup and hand to Thee I hold.

And yet Thou givest; thanks, O Lord,
That still my heart with hunger faints!
The day will come when at Thy board
I sit forgetting all my plaints.

If rain must come and winds must blow,
And I pore long o'er dim-seen chart,
Yet, Lord, let not the hunger go,
And keep the faintness at my heart.

George Macdonald

Lord, Hear My Discontent

Lord, hear my discontent; all blank I stand,
A mirror polished by the hand;
Thy sun's beams flash and flame from me—
I cannot help it; here I stand, there he;
To one of them I cannot say,
Go, and on yonder water play.
Not one poor ragged daisy can I fashion—
I do not make the words of this my limping passion.

Thou only thinkest—I am thought;
Me and my thought Thou thinkest. Naught
Am I but as a fountain spout
From which Thy water welleth out.
Thou art the only One, the All in all.
Yet when my soul on Thee doth call
And Thou dost answer out of everywhere,
I, in Thy allness have my perfect share.

George Macdonald

Although George Macdonald left Scotland as a young
man and lived most of his life in England's cities, the
countryside of his birthplace was the setting for his best
stories. A church like this one in Biggar, Scotland, was
likely where Macdonald learned his first religious lessons
and developed his love for the Scottish countryside.

Alfred, Lord Tennyson

Alfred Tennyson was England's most popular poet of the Victorian era. He served as poet laureate of England for forty-two years and was the first Englishman to be knighted in recognition of literary achievement.

Alfred, the fourth of eight sons in a family of twelve children, was born in 1809 in Lincolnshire, England. His father, George Tennyson, although the eldest son of a wealthy landowner, had been disinherited. Left without land or money but with an excellent classical education, George Tennyson became a clergyman, a profession he disliked. Young Alfred's life in the parsonage was far from idyllic. His father was a drunkard; but in spite of his drinking, Reverend Tennyson still managed to give his sons enough learning so that they could obtain a university education. While still at home, Alfred and one of his brothers published a volume of poetry.

At Cambridge, Tennyson's schoolmate, Arthur Hallam, saw something special in his friend's verses and invited Tennyson to join a student literary club called "The Apostles." Hallam became Tennyson's confidant and friend as well as his sister's fiance; yet the friendship was short-lived. Hallam died suddenly, only a few short years after their meeting. His death devastated Tennyson, who sunk into deep despair. But he never stopped writing. Tennyson took seventeen years to work through the grief he felt for his friend. The result of his pain was "In Memoriam," which details how his years of personal grief strengthened his faith in God. The poem established Tennyson as the prominent literary figure of the era, and it stands today as a poetic masterpiece.

"In Memoriam" was published in 1850; from that time on, Tennyson lived a peaceful, productive, and prosperous life with his wife and their two sons. Hallam's death not only forced Tennyson to find meaning in tragedy but also to reflect on man's relationship to God and to nature. From tragic and humble beginnings, this greatest poet of the Victorian era, and one of the most respected of all time, died in 1892 and now lies with kings and princes in London's Westminster Abbey.

from In Memoriam

Ring out the old, ring in the new,
Ring, happy bells, across the snow:
The year is going, let him go;
Ring out the false, ring in the true.

Ring out the grief that saps the mind,
For those that here we see no more;
Ring out the feud of rich and poor,
Ring in redress to all mankind.

Ring out a slowly dying cause,
And ancient forms of party strife;
Ring in the nobler forms of life,
With sweeter manners, purer laws.

Ring out the want, the care, the sin,
The faithless coldness of the times;
Ring out, ring out my mournful rhymes,
But ring the fuller minstrel in.

Ring out false pride in place and blood,
The civic slander and the spite;
Ring in the love of truth and right,
Ring in the common love of good.

Ring out old shapes of foul disease;
Ring out the narrowing lust of gold;
Ring out the thousand wars of old,
Ring in the thousand years of peace.

Ring in the valiant man and free,
The larger heart, the kindlier hand;
Ring out the darkness of the land,
Ring in the Christ that is to be.

Alfred, Lord Tennyson

from In Memoriam

Love is and was my Lord and King,
And in his presence I attend
To hear the tidings of my friend,
Which every hour his courtiers bring.

Love is and was my King and Lord,
And will be, though as yet I keep
Within his court on earth, and sleep
Encompassed by his faithful guard,

And hear at times a sentinel
Who moves about from place to place,
And whispers to the worlds of space,
In the deep night, that all is well.

Alfred, Lord Tennyson

Since Christmas Day in 1066, when William the Con-
queror was crowned king inside its walls, London's Westminster Abbey has been the most important church in
England. The site of royal coronations, marriages, and
burials, the Abbey is also the final resting place for some of
the country's great literary figures, including Alfred, Lord
Tennyson, who rests in the Abbey's Poets' Corner.

Lives of Historical Impact

"Upon this rock
I will build my church
and the gates of hell will
not prevail
against it."

Matthew 16:18

This tiny chapel in Upper Bavaria, Germany, shining its
light through the winter darkness, is symbolic of the many
great men and women who have championed the cause of
Christianity in the face of persecution and hardship.

Martin Luther

Martin Luther, was born in 1483 in Eisleben, Germany; at the age of twenty-four, he became an Augustinian priest. As the years passed, however, he began to believe in salvation by faith rather than by good works. On October 31, 1517, Martin Luther nailed his "95 Theses" to the door of a church in Wittenberg, Germany, and began a reform movement which forever changed history around the world.

During his years in the priesthood, Luther had seen the church grow distant from believers. Services were in Latin, and the Bible was translated only in Latin and Greek, languages few Germans read or understood. There was neither reading of the scriptures nor congregational singing. There was no way for the people to come to God except by the intervening authority of the church.

Luther sought only to reform the church, not separate from it. He believed the church had been corrupted by men who believed in their own authority more than in the sovereignty of God. For Luther, the solution was simple. The authority of men must be replaced by the only true authority: God's word as expressed through scripture.

For the priest's convictions and teachings, the Catholic church excommunicated him. Threatened with arrest and extradition to Rome for trial in 1521, Martin Luther was locked up for his own protection in a castle near Eisenach, Germany. During this year-long exile, he translated the New Testament into German. Upon his release, he returned to Wittenberg and began organizing the church that bears his name.

In addition to his translation of the Bible and theological writings, Luther also composed hymns. As a musician, he knew the power of music to move people, and the hymns he composed were designed for worship. It is his most well-known hymn—the one most identified with the Reformation, the one sung at Luther's funeral in 1546, and the one whose first line is engraved on his tomb—that best sums up his life's creed: "A mighty fortress is our God/A bulwark never failing."

Martin Luther gave the common German people hymns to sing and scriptures to read. Thus equipped, they began the Protestant Reformation.

An Empty Vessel

Behold, Lord, an empty vessel
that needs to be filled.
My Lord, fill it. I am weak in faith;
strengthen thou me. I am cold in love;
warm me and make me fervent
that my love may go out to my neighbor.

I do not have a strong and firm faith;
at times I doubt and am unable
to trust Thee altogether.
O Lord, help me.
Strengthen my faith and trust in Thee.
In Thee I have sealed the treasures of all I have.

I am poor; Thou art rich
and didst come
to be merciful to the poor.
I am a sinner; Thou art merciful and upright.
With me there is an abundance of sin;
in Thee is the fullness of righteousness.

Therefore, I will remain with Thee
of whom I can receive
but to whom I may not give.
Amen.

Martin Luther

Stand by Me

Do You, my God, stand by me,
against all the world's wisdom and reason. . . .
Not mine, but Yours is the cause. . . .
I would prefer to have peaceful days
and to be out of this turmoil.
But Yours, O Lord, is this cause;
it is righteous and eternal.

Stand by me, You true Eternal God!
In no man do I trust. . . .
Stand by me, O God,
in the name of Your dear son Jesus Christ,
who shall be my defense and shelter,
yes, my mighty fortress,
through all the might and strength
of Your Holy Spirit.
Amen.

Martin Luther

Martin Luther preached at this church, known as Parish Church, in Wittenberg, Germany. It was at another of Wittenberg's churches, Castle Church, that Luther posted the ninety-five theses that began the revolt that led to the Protestant Reformation.

St. Francis of Assisi

The man known today as St. Francis was born Giovanni Bernardone in 1182, the son of a wealthy cloth merchant in Assisi, Italy. He lived only forty-four years, but in those years he left a lasting mark on the Christian world. Franciscan orders of monks still exist today, patterning their lives on the model of St. Francis.

Giovanni was twenty years old when he left behind the life of wealth offered by his family and turned his eyes toward God. In 1202, Assisi was at war with the neighboring city of Perugia. Giovanni was called to fight, and soon thereafter taken prisoner. When he was finally released, he was overcome by a serious illness, which transformed him from a happy, outgoing young man content with his comfortable, wealthy life into a troubled and uncertain man searching for a new direction.

Giovanni's searching took him on a pilgrimage to Rome; when he returned to Assisi, he was certain that he must serve God. At a ruined church outside the city, he prayed for direction. Deep in prayer, Giovanni heard a voice telling him "go and repair my house." He interpreted this call to mean the ruined chapel, and he went to his father's warehouse, took as much cloth as he could carry, sold it in the marketplace, and gave the money to the priest at the chapel. When his father learned what he had done, he took him before the bishop for punishment. Seeing his father driven to madness by the loss of some pieces of cloth, Giovanni stripped off his clothes, gave them to his father, and announced that from that day on he would live in poverty and serve only his Father in heaven.

Giovanni took the name Francis and traveled the countryside. Owning only the clothes on his back, Francis became known for his kindness and his love for all of God's creation. He was often sick and near starvation, but he never wavered from his pledge to serve only God. Francis spread the oldest, simplest message of Christianity: the model for our own lives is found in the life of Jesus Christ.

Francis died in 1226 at the age of forty-five. He left very little written material, yet the legacy of his life remains preserved in his few simple prayers and by those who witnessed his works and passed his story from generation to generation.

Canticle of the Sun

O most high, almighty, good Lord God,
to You belong praise, glory, honor, and all blessing!
Praised be my Lord God for all his creatures,
especially for our brother the sun, who brings us the light;
fair is he and shines with very great splendor;
O Lord, he signifies You to us!

Praised be my Lord for our sister the moon,
and for the stars, which He has set
clear and lovely in heaven.
Praised be my Lord for our brother the wind,
and for the air and clouds, calms and all weather
by which You uphold life in all creatures.
Praised be my Lord for our sister water,
who is very serviceable to us and humble
and precious and clean.
Praised be my Lord for our brother fire,
through whom You give us light in the darkness;
and he is bright and pleasant and very mighty and strong.

Praised be my Lord for our mother the earth,
who sustains us and keeps us and brings forth
various fruits and flowers of many colors, and grass.
Praised be my Lord for all those who pardon
one another for His love's sake,
and who endure weakness and tribulation;
blessed are they who shall peaceably endure, for You,
O Most High, will give them a crown.

Blessed are they who are found walking
by Your most holy will,
for the second death shall have no power
to do them harm.
Praise and bless the Lord, and give thanks to Him
and serve Him with great humility.

St. Francis of Assisi

Instrument of Your Peace

Lord, make me an instrument of Your peace.
Where there is hatred, let me sow love,
where there is injury, pardon,
where there is doubt, faith,
where there is despair, hope,
where there is darkness, light,
where there is sadness, joy.

O Divine Master, grant that I may
not so much seek to be consoled as to console,
not so much to be understood as to understand,
not so much to be loved, as to love;
for it is in giving that we receive,
it is in pardoning that we are pardoned,
it is in dying that we awake to eternal life.

St. Francis of Assisi

In 1979, St. Francis was declared the patron saint of ecologists. Such a role is fitting for this saint, whose kindness and charity extended to every aspect of God's creation. The image of St. Francis seen here in a stained glass window from a Seymour, Connecticut, church is a universally recognized tribute to the saint's inspirational lifestyle.

John Wesley

John Wesley's mother did not leave any aspect of her children's education to chance. In all, nineteen children were born to Susanna Wesley and her husband Samuel, an Anglican pastor in the remote country parish of Epworth in Lincolnshire, England. Each of the nine who survived past infancy began lessons with their mother at the age of five. John Wesley, born in 1703, was expected, like the rest of his siblings, to learn the alphabet on his first day of lessons and, within a year or two, to know the New Testament by heart. One night each week, his mother questioned him on spiritual matters. Little time was available for play.

John entered Oxford at the age of sixteen, and his life there was as disciplined as at home. His diary from his Oxford days includes reminders to "Employ all spare hours in religion" and "Avoid curiosity and all useless employments and knowledge."

Wesley's training prepared him for Oxford but did not prepare him for a trip to the colony of Georgia in 1735. Wesley traveled to Georgia at the invitation of a family friend, James Oglethorpe. Oglethorpe opened the settlement of Georgia to released debtors, poor British families, and persecuted Protestants. He invited John Wesley and his brother Charles to serve as missionaries. In Georgia, John Wesley found himself with a congregation with no interest in serving God. In addition, he had doubts about his own spiritual course. On the trip across the Atlantic during a fierce storm, while other passengers wept in fear of shipwreck, a group of Moravians quietly sang hymns. Wesley was impressed by their unshakable faith. In comparison, he found his own faith lacking.

Wesley returned to England, where he lived in a great spiritual crisis, until, while speaking to a Moravian, he experienced a conversion. Faith alone, Wesley realized, was the key to salvation. Without true faith, the rituals and discipline he had perfected throughout his young life were mere empty repetitions. Until his death in 1791, Wesley devoted his days to spreading his new message of salvation through faith. His Methodism taught that true salvation is open to all believers, and that with faith intact, man can endure any hardship.

Resurrection Prayer

O God,
You have glorified
our victorious Savior
with a visible, triumphant
resurrection from the dead,
and ascension into heaven,
where He sits at Your right hand;

Grant, we beg You,
that His triumphs and glories
may ever shine in our eyes,
to make us more clearly see
through His sufferings,
and more courageously endure our own;

being assured by His example,
that if we endeavor
to live and die like Him,
for the advancement of your love
in ourselves and others,
You will raise our bodies again,
and confirming them to His glorious body,
call us above the clouds,
and give us possession
of Your everlasting kingdom.

John Wesley

Prayer

O God,
whose eternal providence has embarked
our souls in our bodies,
not to expect any port of anchorage
on the sea of this world,
to steer directly through it
to Your glorious kingdom,
preserve us from the dangers
that on all sides assault us,
and keep our affections
still fitly disposed to receive
Your holy inspirations,
that being carried strongly forward
by Your holy spirit
we may happily arrive at last
in the haven of our eternal salvation,
through our Lord, Jesus Christ.
Amen.

John Wesley

This stained glass from the Stanford University Chapel in
Palo Alto, California, depicts the image of Jesus closest to
the heart of John Wesley. The central message of Wesley's
Methodism was that salvation is found through looking in
absolute faith to Jesus as our shepherd.

St. Thomas Aquinas

St. Thomas Aquinas is one of religious history's most eloquent writers. Born approximately 1225, as a youth he was the shy, inarticulate son of wealthy and aristocratic Italian parents who protested his reticence. His silence in group discussions, combined with his physical stature, caused his fellow classmates to nickname him "the dumb Sicilian ox."

Upon his announcement to his family that he intended to enter the order of Dominicans, his parents locked him up and kept him a prisoner in their house for fifteen months. As determined as his nickname implies, the young Aquinas endured until his parents released him. He then left the relative luxury of his childhood home, took a vow of poverty, and joined the Dominicans.

The religious life transformed Thomas Aquinas; and as with Paul of Tarsus, he suddenly could articulate the thoughts and insights of his great mind. As a monk, Thomas Aquinas became known as a powerful lecturer and writer, a man of exceptional intellect who met and influenced the greatest minds of his time.

Aquinas believed that the human intellect was a magnificent gift which allowed man to understand God's existence and benevolence. He established a theological school at Cologne and spent much of his life as a teacher in France, Germany, and Italy. Until his death in 1274, Aquinas devoted his life to study and to teaching and inspiring others, all in the service of God.

Thomas Aquinas was canonized in 1323. His essays and treatises are treasured by those who agree with his beliefs and are respected by those who disagree. The words of Aquinas have influenced generations of religious thinkers and philosophers. Through his intellect, Aquinas sought to understand God's existence; through his eloquence, he translated God's love for the world's generations.

Prayer

O Creator past all telling,
You have appointed
from the treasures of Your wisdom
the hierarchies of angels,
disposing them in wondrous order
above the bright heavens,

and have so beautifully set out
all parts of the universe.
You we call the true fount of wisdom
and the noble origin of all things.

Be pleased to shed
on the darkness of mind in which I was born,
the twofold beam of Your light
and warmth to dispel my ignorance and sin.
You make eloquent the tongues of children.

Then instruct my speech
and touch my lips with graciousness.
Make me keen to understand, quick to learn,
able to remember;

make me delicate to interpret and ready to speak,
guide my going in and going forward,
lead home my going forth.
You are true God and true man,
and live forever and ever.

St. Thomas Aquinas

Give Me, O Lord

Give me, O Lord,
a steadfast heart,
which no unworthy affection
may drag downwards.

Give me
an unconquered heart,
which no tribulations can wear out.

Give me
an upright heart,
which no unworthy purpose
may tempt aside.

St. Thomas Aquinas

Imposing Cologne Cathedral is one of many beautiful, ancient buildings in the city of Cologne, Germany. Cologne has been a center for European education and religion since before the days of St. Thomas Aquinas, who came to the German city to found his theological school.

John Calvin

For most of his adult life, John Calvin was the leading voice of the Protestant Reformation. Born in Picardy, France, in 1509, Calvin was not born to revolutionary religious ideas. As a young man, he was a gifted and serious student, and all who knew him believed him to be destined for something extraordinary. His leanings were toward language and literature, and his religious views can best be classified as humanistic. Calvin seemed headed for the quiet, secular life of a writer and scholar.

A mysterious experience in his early twenties interrupted Calvin's career and transformed him from a budding scholar into a crusader for the cause of the Reformation. All that he ever revealed about this experience is that "God subdued my heart . . . to docility by a sudden conversion." Whatever the cause or circumstances, the conversion was as complete and as permanent as it was sudden. God, not man, became the center of Calvin's universe.

In the sixteenth century, the religious world was deeply divided and in need of strong leadership; Calvin stepped naturally into this role. In 1528, Calvin openly declared his acceptance of the doctrines of the Reformation and consequently was banished from Paris five years later. He took refuge in Basel, Switzerland, where he published his now famous *Institutes of the Christian Religion*. From there he went to Geneva, helping to establish a theocratic government and to found an academy where he later taught theology. John Calvin continued writing and teaching until his death in 1564, bringing all the scattered and disorganized opinions of the Reformation into one doctrine known as Calvinism.

John Calvin heard the call for devotion to the service of God, and he answered without hesitation by throwing himself into the midst of one of the greatest upheavals the religious world has ever known. His prayers reveal the central principle that drove him to lead the cause of the Reformation: Christians do not need the church to approach God or to govern their own lives. They simply need God's word as revealed in the scriptures and their own complete devotion to the authority of that word.

A Prayer

Grant, almighty God,
that as You have, in various ways,
testified and daily also proven
how dear and precious to You is humanity,
as we daily enjoy so many and so remarkable
proofs of Your goodness and favor—

O grant that we learn to rely
wholly on Your goodness,
so many examples of which
You set before us,
and which You would have us
continually to experience,
that we may not only
pass through our earthly course,
but also confidently aspire
to the hope of that blessed and celestial life
which is laid up for us in heaven,
through Christ alone our Lord.
Amen.

John Calvin

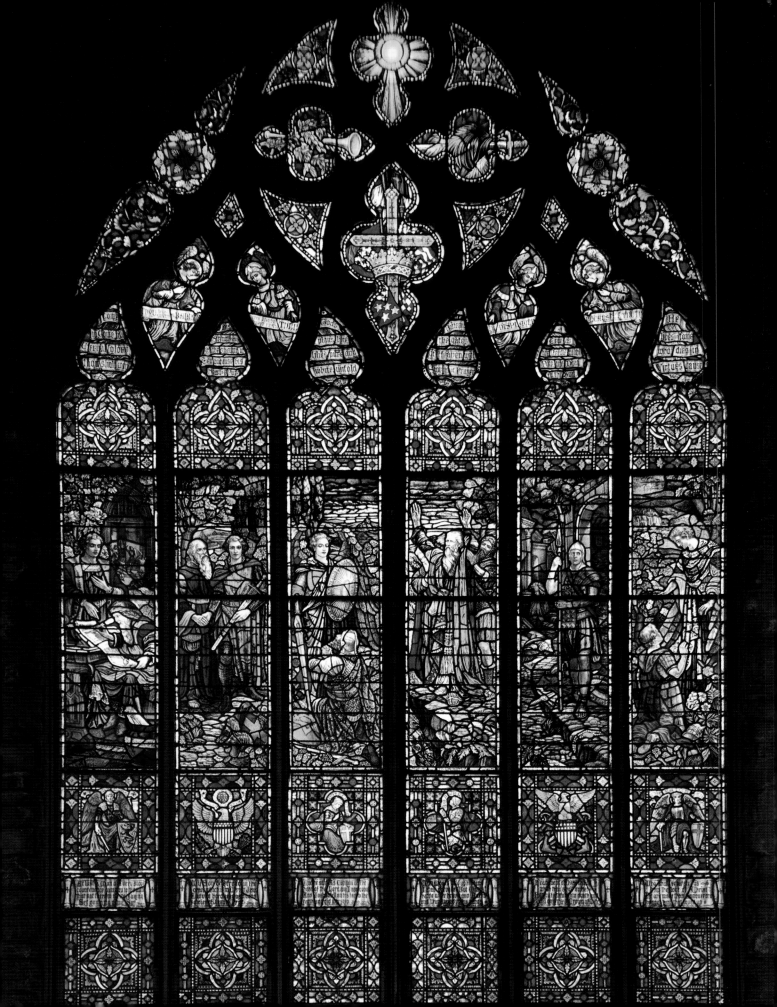

A Morning Prayer

Grant, almighty God,
that as You shine on us by Your word,
we may not be blind at midday,
nor willfully see darkness,
and thus lull our minds asleep:

but, may we be roused daily by Your words,
and may we stir up ourselves
more and more to fear Your name
and thus present ourselves and all our pursuits,
as a sacrifice to You, that You may peaceably rule
and perpetually dwell in us until You gather us
to Your celestial habitation,

where there is reserved for us
eternal rest and glory,
through Jesus Christ our Lord.
Amen.

John Calvin

The First Presbyterian Church in Lansdowne, Pennsylvania, that houses this wonderful stained glass window has its roots in the sixteenth-century teachings of John Calvin. Calvinism was also the theology behind the Congregational churches of the first Puritan settlers of New England.

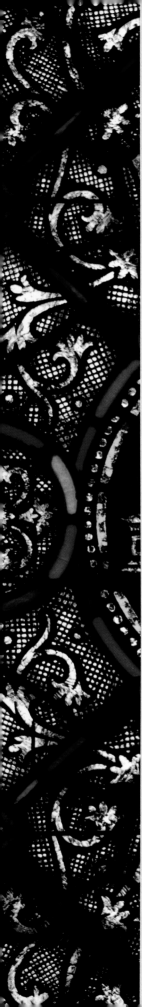

St. Augustine

For more than thirty years of his life, the man who would one day be known as St. Augustine lived a life apart from God. Augustine was born in 354 in the country of Numibia, which is now known as Algeria. His father was a Roman official and a pagan; his mother was a devout Christian. Augustine was not baptized as a child, and he received little religious instruction. He had an active, searching mind, and as a young man sought the answers to life's questions through philosophy and worldly experience. But nothing satisfied him, neither philosophical rhetoric nor sensual pleasures.

After completing his education, Augustine turned to teaching. Between the years 373 and 387, he taught grammar and rhetoric and also fathered a son by his mistress. Throughout these years, Augustine rejected the answers offered by Christianity but still remained troubled by the lack of meaning in his own life. One day, as he sat in a garden pondering the direction of his life, he heard a voice urging him to read Paul's letter to the Romans. There Augustine found an end to his searching. He took Paul's words to heart: "Not in revelling and drunkenness, nor in lust or wantonness, not in quarrels and rivalries. Rather arm yourself with the Lord Jesus Christ." Through these words Augustine found peace for the first time in his life. On April 25, 387, he and his son were baptized.

After his baptism, Augustine sold all that he owned, distributed the money to the poor, and established a monastic community. Augustine was later ordained a priest and eventually became the bishop of the city of Hippo. Regardless of his position, his goal remained the same. Through preaching, writing, and example, Augustine sought to spread the message that God is man's only refuge and the source of all knowledge and good.

Augustine died in 430. His *Confessions*, which tells the story of his early life of sin and suffering, and his other works on practically every aspect of Christian thought and church doctrine have influenced the great Christian minds of every century since his death. Augustine, a man who took years to open his heart to God, is today considered one of the greatest Christian voices in history.

A Prayer

Blessed are all Your saints,
O God and King, who have traveled
over the tempestuous sea of this life
and have made the harbor of peace and felicity.

Watch over us
who are still on our dangerous voyage;
and remember those who lie exposed to
the rough storms of trouble and temptations.

Frail is our vessel, and the ocean is wide;
but as in Your memory You have set our course,
so steer the vessel of our life towards
the everlasting shore of peace,
and bring us at length
to the quiet haven of our heart's desire,
where You, O God,
are blessed and live and reign forever.

St. Augustine

Hide Not Thy Face

Oh! that I might repose on Thee!
Oh! that Thou wouldest enter into my heart,
and inebriate it, that I may forget my ills,
and embrace Thee, my sole good!

What art Thou to me?
In Thy pity, teach me to utter it.
Or what am I to Thee that Thou demandest my love,
and if I give it not, art wroth with me,
and threatenest me with grievous woes?

Is it then a light woe to love Thee not?
Oh, for Thy mercies' sake, tell me, O Lord, my God,
what Thou art unto me.
Say unto my soul, I am thy salvation.
So speak that I may hear.

Behold, Lord, my heart is before Thee;
open Thou the ears thereof, and say unto my soul,
I am thy salvation.
After this voice let me haste,
and take hold on Thee.
Hide not Thy face from me.

St. Augustine

After his conversion at age thirty-three, St. Augustine worked tirelessly to spread and defend the Catholic church. Today his writings and the story of his life remain an important part of Catholic tradition. The Vatican's Sistine Chapel is another lasting piece of Catholic culture. Built in the fifteenth century, the Sistine Chapel is adorned by Michelangelo's frescoes, which are universally acknowledged as timeless masterpieces of art.

Poem and Prayer Index

Subject Index

Biography Index

Photographs